MznLnx

Missing Links Exam Preps

Exam Prep for

Calculus with Applications

Lial, Greenwell, Ritchey, 8th Edition

The MznLnx Exam Prep is your link from the textbook and lecture to your exams.
The MznLnx Exam Preps are unauthorized and comprehensive reviews of your textbooks.

All material provided by MznLnx and Rico Publications (c) 2010
Textbook publishers and textbook authors do not particpate in or contribute to these reviews.

MznLnx

Rico
Publications

Exam Prep for Calculus with Applications
8th Edition
Lial, Greenwell, Ritchey

Publisher: Raymond Houge
Assistant Editor: Michael Rouger
Text and Cover Designer: Lisa Buckner
Marketing Manager: Sara Swagger
Project Manager, Editorial Production: Jerry Emerson
Art Director: Vernon Lowerui

Product Manager: Dave Mason
Editorial Assitant: Rachel Guzmanji
Pedagogy: Debra Long
Cover Image: Jim Reed/Getty Images
Text and Cover Printer: City Printing, Inc.
Compositor: Media Mix, Inc.

(c) 2010 Rico Publications
ALL RIGHTS RESERVED. No part of this work covered by the copyright may be reproduced or used in any form or by an means--graphic, electronic, or mechanical, including photocopying, recording, taping, Web distribution, information storage, and retrieval systems, or in any other manner--without the written permission of the publisher.

For more information about our products, contact us at:
Dave.Mason@RicoPublications.com

For permission to use material from this text or product, submit a request online to:
Dave.Mason@RicoPublications.com

Printed in the United States
ISBN:

Contents

CHAPTER 1
LINEAR FUNCTIONS   1
CHAPTER 2
NONLINEAR FUNCTIONS   8
CHAPTER 3
THE DERIVATIVE   24
CHAPTER 4
CALCULATING THE DERIVATIVE   34
CHAPTER 5
GRAPHS AND THE DERIVATIVE   43
CHAPTER 6
APPLICATIONS OF THE DERIVATIVE   55
CHAPTER 7
INTEGRATION   62
CHAPTER 8
FURTHER TECHNIQUES AND APPLICATIONS OF INTEGRATION   74
CHAPTER 9
MULTIVARIABLE CALCULUS   80
CHAPTER 10
DIFFERENTIAL EQUATIONS   94
CHAPTER 11
PROBABILITY AND CALCULUS   102
CHAPTER 12
SEQUENCES AND SERIES   107
CHAPTER 13
THE TRIGONOMETRIC FUNCTIONS   113
ANSWER KEY   118

TO THE STUDENT

COMPREHENSIVE

The *MznLnx* Exam Prep series is designed to help you pass your exams. Editors at MznLnx review your textbooks and then prepare these practice exams to help you master the textbook material. Unlike study guides, workbooks, and practice tests provided by the texbook publisher and textbook authors, *MznLnx* gives you **all** of the material in each chapter in exam form, not just samples, so you can be sure to nail your exam.

MECHANICAL

The MznLnx Exam Prep series creates exams that will help you learn the subject matter as well as test you on your understanding. Each question is designed to help you master the concept. Just working through the exams, you gain an understanding of the subject--its a simple mechanical process that produces success.

INTEGRATED STUDY GUIDE AND REVIEW

MznLnx is not just a set of exams designed to test you, its also a comprehensive review of the subject content. Each exam question is also a review of the concept, making sure that you will get the answer correct without having to go to other sources of material. You learn as you go! Its the easiest way to pass an exam.

HUMOR

Studying can be tedious and dry. MznLnx's instructional design includes moderate humor within the exam questions on occassion, to break the tedium and revitalize the brain

Chapter 1. LINEAR FUNCTIONS

1. In mathematics, the _____ is used to determine each point uniquely in a plane through two numbers, usually called the x-coordinate or abscissa and the y-coordinate or ordinate of the point. To define the coordinates, two perpendicular directed lines, are specified, as well as the unit length, which is marked off on the two axes Cartesian coordinate systems are also used in space and in higher dimensions.

   a. Coordinate
   b. Cartesian coordinate system
   c. 15 theorem
   d. Cylindrical coordinate system

2. In mathematics and its applications, a _____ system is a system for assigning an n-tuple of numbers or scalars to each point in an n-dimensional space. This concept is part of the theory of manifolds. 'Scalars' in many cases means real numbers, but, depending on context, can mean complex numbers or elements of some other commutative ring.

   a. 15 theorem
   b. Cylindrical coordinate system
   c. Spherical coordinate system
   d. Coordinate

3. In metric topology and related fields of mathematics, a set U is called _____ if, intuitively speaking, starting from any point x in U one can move by a small amount in any direction and still be in the set U. In other words, the distance between any point x in U and the edge of U is always greater than zero.

   As an example, consider the _____ interval (0, 1) consisting of all real numbers x with 0 < x < 1. Here, the topology is the usual topology on the real line. We can look at this in two ways.

   a. AUSM
   b. ACTRAN
   c. ALGOR
   d. Open

4. The _____ of any solid, liquid, plasma, vacuum or theoretical object is how much three-dimensional space it occupies, often quantified numerically. One-dimensional figures (such as lines) and two-dimensional shapes (such as squares) are assigned zero _____ in the three-dimensional space. _____ is commonly presented in units such as mL or cm^3 (milliliters or cubic centimeters.)

   a. Klein-Gordon equation
   b. Vector potential
   c. Dirac equation
   d. Volume

Chapter 1. LINEAR FUNCTIONS

5. Just as the definite integral of a positive function of one variable represents the area of the region between the graph of the function and the x-axis, the _____ of a positive function of two variables represents the volume of the region between the surface defined by the function (on the three dimensional Cartesian plane where z = f(x,y)) and the plane which contains its domain. (Note that the same volume can be obtained via the triple integral -- the integral of a function in three variables -- of the constant function f(x, y, z) = 1 over the above-mentioned region between the surface and the plane.) If there are more variables, a multiple integral will yield hypervolumes of multi-dimensional functions.
   a. Risch algorithm
   b. Trigonometric substitution
   c. Constant of integration
   d. Double integral

6. Integration is an important concept in mathematics, specifically in the field of calculus and, more broadly, mathematical analysis. Given a function f of a real variable x and an interval [a, b] of the real line, the _____

$$\int_a^b f(x)\, dx,$$

is defined informally to be the net signed area of the region in the xy-plane bounded by the graph of f, the x-axis, and the vertical lines x = a and x = b.

The term '_____' may also refer to the notion of antiderivative, a function F whose derivative is the given function f.

   a. Integral test for convergence
   b. Integrand
   c. Integral
   d. Indefinite integral

7. In computer science and information science, _____ could also be a method or an algorithm. Again, an example will illustrate: There are systems of counting, as with Roman numerals, and various systems for filing papers, or catalogues, and various library systems, of which the Dewey Decimal _____ is an example. This still fits with the definition of components which are connected together (in this case in order to facilitate the flow of information.)
   a. BIBO stability
   b. BDDC
   c. System
   d. 15 theorem

Chapter 1. LINEAR FUNCTIONS

8. _____ is used to describe the steepness, incline, gradient, or grade of a straight line. A higher _____ value indicates a steeper incline. The _____ is defined as the ratio of the 'rise' divided by the 'run' between two points on a line, or in other words, the ratio of the altitude change to the horizontal distance between any two points on the line.

   a. 15 theorem
   b. Y-intercept
   c. Sequence
   d. Slope

9. In coordinate geometry, the _____ is the y-value of the point where the graph of a function or relation intercepts the y-axis of the coordinate system.

In other words, the _____ of a function is the y-value of the point at which it intersects the line x=0 (the y-axis.) Thus, if the function is specified in form y = f(x), the _____ is easy to find by calculating f.

   a. Slope
   b. Sequence
   c. 15 theorem
   d. Y-intercept

10. In infinitesimal calculus, a _____ is traditionally an infinitesimally small change in a variable. For example, if x is a variable, then a change in the value of x is often denoted Δx (or δx when this change is considered to be small.) The _____ dx represents such a change, but is infinitely small.

   a. The Method of Mechanical Theorems
   b. Dirichlet integral
   c. Local maximum
   d. Differential

11. A _____ is a mathematical equation for an unknown function of one or several variables that relates the values of the function itself and of its derivatives of various orders. they play a prominent role in engineering, physics, economics and other disciplines.

A simplified real world example of a _____ is modeling the acceleration of a ball falling through the air (considering only gravity and air resistance.)

   a. Phase line
   b. Differential equation
   c. Structural stability
   d. Caloric polynomial

Chapter 1. LINEAR FUNCTIONS

12. A _____ is an algebraic equation in which each term is either a constant or the product of a constant and (the first power of) a single variable. Linear equations can have one, two, three or more variables. Linear equations occur with great regularity in applied mathematics.

   a. Quadratic formula
   b. Quartic function
   c. Cubic function
   d. Linear equation

13. The terms '_____' and 'independent variable' are used in similar but subtly different ways in mathematics and statistics as part of the standard terminology in those subjects. They are used to distinguish between two types of quantities being considered, separating them into those available at the start of a process and those being created by it, where the latter (dependent variables) are dependent on the former (independent variables.)

In traditional calculus, a function is defined as a relation between two terms called variables because their values vary.

   a. 15 theorem
   b. BDDC
   c. BIBO stability
   d. Dependent variable

14. The terms 'dependent variable' and '_____' are used in similar but subtly different ways in mathematics and statistics as part of the standard terminology in those subjects. They are used to distinguish between two types of quantities being considered, separating them into those available at the start of a process and those being created by it, where the latter (dependent variables) are dependent on the former (independent variables.)

In traditional calculus, a function is defined as a relation between two terms called variables because their values vary.

   a. AUSM
   b. ACTRAN
   c. ALGOR
   d. Independent variable

15. In mathematics, a (topological) _____ is defined as follows: let I be an interval of real numbers (i.e. a non-empty connected subset of $\mathbb{R}$); then a _____ γ is a continuous mapping $\gamma : I \to X$, where X is a topological space. The _____ γ is said to be simple if it is injective, i.e. if for all x, y in I, we have $\gamma(x) = \gamma(y) \implies x = y$. If I is a closed bounded interval $[a, b]$, we also allow the possibility $\gamma(a) = \gamma(b)$ (this convention makes it possible to talk about closed simple _____.)

Chapter 1. LINEAR FUNCTIONS

a. Prolate cycloid
b. Curve
c. Closed curve
d. Tractrix

16. The method of _____ or ordinary _____ is used to solve overdetermined systems. _____ is often applied in statistical contexts, particularly regression analysis.

_____ can be interpreted as a method of fitting data. The best fit in the _____ sense is that instance of the model for which the sum of squared residuals has its least value, a residual being the difference between an observed value and the value given by the model.

a. Least squares
b. BDDC
c. 15 theorem
d. BIBO stability

17. Trigonometry is a branch of mathematics that deals with triangles, particularly those plane triangles in which one angle has 90 degrees (right triangles.) Trigonometry deals with relationships between the sides and the angles of triangles and with the _____ functions, which describe those relationships.

Trigonometry has applications in both pure mathematics and in applied mathematics, where it is essential in many branches of science and technology.

a. Trigonometric
b. Sine
c. Trigonometric integrals
d. Trigonometric functions

18. In mathematics, the _____ are functions of an angle. They are important in the study of triangles and modeling periodic phenomena, among many other applications. _____ are commonly defined as ratios of two sides of a right triangle containing the angle, and can equivalently be defined as the lengths of various line segments from a unit circle.

a. Trigonometric integrals
b. Trigonometric functions
c. Trigonometric
d. Sine integral

19. In mathematics, the simplest case of _____ refers to the study of problems in which one seeks to minimize or maximize a real function by systematically choosing the values of real or integer variables from within an allowed set. This (a scalar real valued objective function) is actually a small subset of this field which comprises a large area of applied mathematics and generalizes to study of means to obtain 'best available' values of some objective function given a defined domain where the elaboration is on the types of functions and the conditions and nature of the objects in the problem domain.

The first _____ technique, which is known as steepest descent, goes back to Gauss.

a. AUSM
b. Optimization
c. ALGOR
d. ACTRAN

20. _____ is the addition of a set of numbers; the result is their sum or total. An interim or present total of a _____ process is termed the running total. The 'numbers' to be summed may be natural numbers, complex numbers, matrices, or still more complicated objects.

a. Summation
b. 15 theorem
c. BIBO stability
d. BDDC

21. In calculus, a branch of mathematics, the _____ is a measurement of how a function changes when its input changes. Loosely speaking, a _____ can be thought of as how much a quantity is changing at some given point. For example, the _____ of the position (or distance) of a vehicle with respect to time is the instantaneous velocity (respectively, instantaneous speed) at which the vehicle is traveling.

The process of finding a _____ is called differentiation. The fundamental theorem of calculus states that differentiation is the reverse process to integration.

a. Semi-differentiability
b. Stationary phase approximation
c. Bounded function
d. Derivative

22. In mathematics, a _____ is a constant multiplicative factor of a certain object. For example, in the expression $9x^2$, the _____ of x^2 is 9.

The object can be such things as a variable, a vector, a function, etc.

a. Coefficient
b. Resultant
c. Degree of the polynomial
d. Binomial type

23. In probability theory and statistics, _____ indicates the strength and direction of a linear relationship between two random variables. That is in contrast with the usage of the term in colloquial speech, denoting any relationship, not necessarily linear. In general statistical usage, _____ or co-relation refers to the departure of two random variables from independence.
   a. Correlation
   b. Geometric mean
   c. Standard deviation
   d. Continuous random variable

Chapter 2. NONLINEAR FUNCTIONS

1. In calculus, an _____, primitive or indefinite integral of a function f is a function F whose derivative is equal to f, i.e., F >' = f. The process of solving for antiderivatives is antidifferentiation (or indefinite integration.) Antiderivatives are related to definite integrals through the fundamental theorem of calculus: the definite integral of a function over an interval is equal to the difference between the values of an _____ evaluated at the endpoints of the interval.
    a. Integrand
    b. Antiderivative
    c. Indefinite integral
    d. Order of integration

2. In mathematics, the simplest case of _____ refers to the study of problems in which one seeks to minimize or maximize a real function by systematically choosing the values of real or integer variables from within an allowed set. This (a scalar real valued objective function) is actually a small subset of this field which comprises a large area of applied mathematics and generalizes to study of means to obtain 'best available' values of some objective function given a defined domain where the elaboration is on the types of functions and the conditions and nature of the objects in the problem domain.

    The first _____ technique, which is known as steepest descent, goes back to Gauss.

    a. AUSM
    b. Optimization
    c. ALGOR
    d. ACTRAN

3. In mathematics, the _____ (or replacement set) of a given function is the set of 'input' values for which the function is defined. For instance, the _____ of cosine would be all real numbers, while the _____ of the square root would be only numbers greater than or equal to 0 (ignoring complex numbers in both cases.) In a representation of a function in a xy Cartesian coordinate system, the _____ is represented on the x axis (or abscissa.)
    a. BIBO stability
    b. BDDC
    c. 15 theorem
    d. Domain

4. In mathematics, the _____ of a function is the set of all 'output' values produced by that function. Sometimes it is called the image, or more precisely, the image of the domain of the function. If a function is a surjection then its _____ is equal to its codomain.
    a. Constant function
    b. Piecewise-defined function
    c. Surjective
    d. Range

Chapter 2. NONLINEAR FUNCTIONS

5. The terms 'dependent variable' and '_____' are used in similar but subtly different ways in mathematics and statistics as part of the standard terminology in those subjects. They are used to distinguish between two types of quantities being considered, separating them into those available at the start of a process and those being created by it, where the latter (dependent variables) are dependent on the former (independent variables.)

In traditional calculus, a function is defined as a relation between two terms called variables because their values vary.

   a. ACTRAN
   b. ALGOR
   c. AUSM
   d. Independent variable

6. _____ is a type of motion in which the velocity of an object changes equal amounts in equal time periods. An example of an object having _____ would be a ball rolling down a ramp. The object picks up velocity as it goes down the ramp with equal changes in time.
   a. AUSM
   b. ALGOR
   c. ACTRAN
   d. Uniform Acceleration

7. In mathematics, a _____ is a function whose values do not vary and thus are constant. For example, if we have the function f(x) = 4, then f is constant since f maps any value to 4. More formally, a function f : A → B is a _____ if f(x) = f(y) for all x and y in A.
   a. Surjective
   b. Range
   c. Piecewise-defined function
   d. Constant function

8. The _____ is a test to determine if a relation or its graph is a function or not. For a relation or graph to be a function, it can have at most a single y-value for each x-value. Thus, a vertical line drawn at any x-position on the graph of a function will intersect the graph at most once.
   a. 15 theorem
   b. BIBO stability
   c. BDDC
   d. Vertical line test

Chapter 2. NONLINEAR FUNCTIONS

9. In mathematics, a function on the real numbers is called a _____ (or staircase function) if it can be written as a finite linear combination of indicator functions of intervals. Informally speaking, a _____ is a piecewise constant function having only finitely many pieces.

    a. Square root function
    b. Multiplicative inverse
    c. Hyperbolic sine
    d. Step function

10. In mathematics, the _____ is a conic section, the intersection of a right circular conical surface and a plane parallel to a generating straight line of that surface. Given a point (the focus) and a line (the directrix) that lie in a plane, the locus of points in that plane that are equidistant to them is a _____.

    A particular case arises when the plane is tangent to the conical surface of a circle.

    a. 15 theorem
    b. BIBO stability
    c. BDDC
    d. Parabola

11. In mathematics, a _____ is a polynomial equation of the second degree. The general form is

    $$ax^2 + bx + c = 0,$$

    where a ≠ 0.

    Students and teachers all over the world are familiar with the quadratic formula that can be derived by completing the square.

    a. Stern-Brocot tree
    b. Quadratic equation
    c. Continued fraction
    d. Lochs' theorem

12. A quadratic equation with real or complex coefficients has two solutions (or roots), not necessarily distinct, which may or may not be real, given by the _____:

$$\frac{-b \pm \sqrt{b^2 - 4ac}}{2a}$$

Example discriminant signsâ— <0: $x^2+½â—$ =0: $-\frac{4}{3}x^2+\frac{4}{3}x-\frac{1}{3}â—$ >0: $\frac{3}{2}x^2+\frac{1}{2}x-\frac{4}{3}$

In the above formula, the expression underneath the square root sign

$$D = b^2 - 4ac,$$

is called the discriminant of the quadratic equation.

A quadratic equation with real coefficients can have either one or two distinct real roots, or two distinct complex roots. In this case the discriminant determines the number and nature of the roots.

a. Linear equation
b. Cubic function
c. Quartic function
d. Quadratic formula

13. A _____, in mathematics, is a polynomial function of the form $f(x) = ax^2 + bx + c$, where $a \neq 0$. The graph of a _____ is a parabola whose major axis is parallel to the y-axis.

The expression $ax^2 + bx + c$ in the definition of a _____ is a polynomial of degree 2 or a 2nd degree polynomial, because the highest exponent of x is 2.

a. Leading coefficient
b. Discriminant
c. Resultant
d. Quadratic function

14. In physics, _____ is movement that changes the position of an object, as opposed to rotation. For example, according to Whittaker:

A _____ is the operation changing the positions of all points (x, y, z) of an object according to the formula

$$(x, y, z) \to (x + \Delta x, y + \Delta y, z + \Delta z)$$

where $(\Delta x, \Delta y, \Delta z)$ is the same vector for each point of the object. The _____ vector $(\Delta x, \Delta y, \Delta z)$ common to all points of the object describes a particular type of displacement of the object, usually called a linear displacement to distinguish it from displacements involving rotation, called angular displacements.

a. BDDC
b. 15 theorem
c. BIBO stability
d. Translation

15. In elementary algebra, _____ is a technique for converting a quadratic polynomial of the form

$$ax^2 + bx + c$$

to the form

$$a(\cdots\cdots)^2 + \text{constant}.$$

The expression inside the parenthesis is of the form x − constant. Thus one converts ax² + bx + c to

$$a(x - h)^2 + k$$

and one must find h and k.

_____ is used in

- solving quadratic equations,
- graphing quadratic functions,
- evaluating integrals in calculus,
- finding Laplace transforms.

In mathematics, _____ is considered a basic algebraic operation, and is often applied without remark in any computation involving quadratic polynomials.

There is a simple formula in elementary algebra for computing the square of a binomial:

$$(x + p)^2 = x^2 + 2px + p^2.$$

For example:

$$(x+3)^2 = x^2 + 6x + 9 \quad (p=3)$$
$$(x-5)^2 = x^2 - 10x + 25 \quad (p=-5).$$

In any perfect square, the number p is always half the coefficient of x, and then the constant term is equal to p^2.

a. Multinomial theorem
b. Closed-form expression
c. Hurwitz quaternion order
d. Completing the square

16. In mathematics, the _____ is a representation of a function as an infinite sum of terms calculated from the values of its derivatives at a single point. It may be regarded as the limit of the Taylor polynomials. If the series is centered at zero, the series is also called a Maclaurin series.

a. BDDC
b. BIBO stability
c. Taylor series
d. 15 theorem

17. In mathematics, a _____ is a constant multiplicative factor of a certain object. For example, in the expression $9x^2$, the _____ of x^2 is 9.

The object can be such things as a variable, a vector, a function, etc.

a. Degree of the polynomial
b. Coefficient
c. Resultant
d. Binomial type

18. For the largest k where $a_k \neq 0$, a_k is called the _____ of P because most often, polynomials are written starting from the left with the largest power of x. So for example the _____ of the polynomial

$$4x^5 + x^3 + 2x^2$$

is 4.

Chapter 2. NONLINEAR FUNCTIONS

The coefficients of polynomial also may be in the other order:

$$Q(x) = a_0 x^k + a_1 x^{k-1} + \cdots + a_{k-1} x^1 + a_k$$

and must be $a_0 \neq 0$ and a_0 is the _____ of Q.

a. Resultant
b. Leading coefficient
c. Discriminant
d. Symmetric function

19. In mathematics and elsewhere, the adjective _____ means 'fourth order', such as the function x^4. A _____ number is a number which equals the fourth power of an integer.

a. 15 theorem
b. BDDC
c. Reduction
d. Quartic

20. In mathematics, a _____ is a function of the form

$$f(x) = ax^4 + bx^3 + cx^2 + dx + e$$

where a is nonzero; or in other words, a polynomial of degree of four. Such a function is sometimes called a biquadratic function, but the latter term can occasionally also refer to a quadratic function of a square, having the form

$$ax^4 + bx^2 + c,$$

or a product of two quadratic factors, having the form

$$(ax^2 + bx + c)(dy^2 + ey + f).$$

If you set f(x) = 0, you get a quartic equation of the form:

$$ax^4 + bx^3 + cx^2 + dx + e = 0$$

where $a \neq 0$.

The derivative of a _____ is a cubic function.

a. Linear equation
b. Quadratic formula
c. Cubic function
d. Quartic function

21. In mathematics, _____ and minima, known collectively as extrema, are the largest value (maximum) or smallest value (minimum), that a function takes in a point either within a given neighbourhood (local extremum) or on the function domain in its entirety (global extremum.)

Throughout, a point refers to an input (x), while a value refers to an output (y): one distinguishing between the maximum value and the point (or points) at which it occurs.

A real-valued function f defined on the real line is said to have a local maximum point at the point x^*, if there exists some $\varepsilon > 0$, such that $f(x^*) \geq f(x)$ when $|x - x^*| < \varepsilon$.

a. Leibniz formula
b. Racetrack principle
c. Related rates
d. Maxima

22. In mathematics, a _____ is any function which can be written as the ratio of two polynomial functions.

$$y = \frac{x^2 - 3x - 2}{x^2 - 4}$$

In the case of one variable, x, a _____ is a function of the form

$$f(x) = \frac{P(x)}{Q(x)}$$

where P and Q are polynomial function in x and Q is not the zero polynomial. The domain of f is the set of all points x for which the denominator Q(x) is not zero.

a. BDDC
b. 15 theorem
c. BIBO stability
d. Rational function

23. An _____ of a real-valued function y = f(x) is a curve which describes the behavior of f as either x or y tends to infinity.

In other words, as one moves along the graph of f(x) in some direction, the distance between it and the _____ eventually becomes smaller than any distance that one may specify.

a. ALGOR
b. ACTRAN
c. AUSM
d. Asymptote

24. Suppose f is a function. Then the line y = a is a _____ for f if

$$\lim_{x \to \infty} f(x) = a \text{ or } \lim_{x \to -\infty} f(x) = a.$$

Intuitively, this means that f(x) can be made as close as desired to a by making x big enough. How big is big enough depends on how close one wishes to make f(x) to a.

a. Third derivative
b. Mountain pass theorem
c. Second derivative
d. Horizontal asymptote

25. The line x = a is a _____ of a curve y=f(x) if at least one of the following statements is true:

1. $\lim_{x \to a} f(x) = \pm\infty$
2. $\lim_{x \to a^-} f(x) = \pm\infty$
3. $\lim_{x \to a^+} f(x) = \pm\infty$

Intuitively, if x = a is an asymptote of f, then, if we imagine x approaching a from one side, the value of f(x) grows without bound; i.e., f(x) becomes large (positively or negatively), and, in fact, becomes larger than any finite value.

Note that f(x) may or may not be defined at a: what the function is doing precisely at x = a does not affect the asymptote. For example, consider the function

$$f(x) = \begin{cases} \frac{1}{x} & \text{if } x > 0, \\ 5 & \text{if } x \leq 0 \end{cases}$$

As $\lim_{x \to 0^+} f(x) = \infty$, f(x) has a _____ at 0, even though f(0) = 5.

Another example is $f(x) = 1/(x-1)$ which has a _____ of x=1 as shown by the limit

$$\lim_{x \to 1^+} \frac{1}{x-1} = \infty$$

In the graph of $f(x) = x + \frac{1}{x}$, the y-axis (x = 0) and the line y = x are both asymptotes.

When a linear asymptote is not parallel to the x- or y-axis, it is called either an oblique asymptote or equivalently a slant asymptote.

a. Vertical asymptote
b. Third derivative
c. Ramp function
d. Monodromy

26. In economics, _____ is equal to total cost divided by the number of goods produced (the output quantity, Q.) It is also equal to the sum of average variable costs (total variable costs divided by Q) plus average fixed costs (total fixed costs divided by Q.) Average costs may be dependent on the time period considered (increasing production may be expensive or impossible in the short term, for example.)

a. AUSM
b. ALGOR
c. ACTRAN
d. Average cost

27. The _____ is a function in mathematics. The application of this function to a value x is written as exp(x). Equivalently, this can be written in the form e^x, where e is a mathematical constant, the base of the natural logarithm, which equals approximately 2.718281828, and is also known as Euler's number.

Chapter 2. NONLINEAR FUNCTIONS

a. Area hyperbolic functions
b. Integral part
c. ACTRAN
d. Exponential function

28. _____ is the concept of adding accumulated interest back to the principal, so that interest is earned on interest from that moment on. The act of declaring interest to be principal is called compounding (i.e., interest is compounded.) A loan, for example, may have its interest compounded every month: in this case, a loan with $100 principal and 1% interest per month would have a balance of $101 at the end of the first month.

a. 15 theorem
b. BDDC
c. Compound interest
d. BIBO stability

29. In infinitesimal calculus, a _____ is traditionally an infinitesimally small change in a variable. For example, if x is a variable, then a change in the value of x is often denoted Δx (or δx when this change is considered to be small.) The _____ dx represents such a change, but is infinitely small.

a. Differential
b. The Method of Mechanical Theorems
c. Local maximum
d. Dirichlet integral

30. A _____ is a mathematical equation for an unknown function of one or several variables that relates the values of the function itself and of its derivatives of various orders. they play a prominent role in engineering, physics, economics and other disciplines.

A simplified real world example of a _____ is modeling the acceleration of a ball falling through the air (considering only gravity and air resistance.)

a. Differential equation
b. Caloric polynomial
c. Phase line
d. Structural stability

31. In a totally ordered set all elements are mutually comparable, so such a set can have at most one minimal element and at most one maximal element. Then, due to mutual comparability, the minimal element will also be the least element and the maximal element will also be the greatest element. Thus in a totally ordered set we can simply use the terms minimum and _____.

Chapter 2. NONLINEAR FUNCTIONS

a. Maximum
b. Nth term
c. Racetrack principle
d. Leibniz rule

32. In calculus, the _____ is a formula for the derivative of the composite of two functions.

In intuitive terms, if a variable, y, depends on a second variable, u, which in turn depends on a third variable, x, then the rate of change of y with respect to x can be computed as the rate of change of y with respect to u multiplied by the rate of change of u with respect to x. Schematically,

$$\frac{dy}{dx} = \frac{dy}{du} \cdot \frac{du}{dx}.$$

a. Product rule
b. Differentiation rules
c. Reciprocal Rule
d. Chain rule

33. _____ (including exponential decay) occurs when the growth rate of a mathematical function is proportional to the function's current value. In the case of a discrete domain of definition with equal intervals it is also called geometric growth or geometric decay (the function values form a geometric progression.)

_____ is said to follow an exponential law; the simple-_____ model is known as the Malthusian growth model.

a. Inseparable differential equation
b. Oscillating
c. Isomonodromic deformation
d. Exponential growth

34. The _____ of any solid, liquid, plasma, vacuum or theoretical object is how much three-dimensional space it occupies, often quantified numerically. One-dimensional figures (such as lines) and two-dimensional shapes (such as squares) are assigned zero _____ in the three-dimensional space. _____ is commonly presented in units such as mL or cm^3 (milliliters or cubic centimeters.)

a. Dirac equation
b. Volume
c. Vector potential
d. Klein-Gordon equation

35. Just as the definite integral of a positive function of one variable represents the area of the region between the graph of the function and the x-axis, the _____ of a positive function of two variables represents the volume of the region between the surface defined by the function (on the three dimensional Cartesian plane where z = f(x,y)) and the plane which contains its domain. (Note that the same volume can be obtained via the triple integral -- the integral of a function in three variables -- of the constant function f(x, y, z) = 1 over the above-mentioned region between the surface and the plane.) If there are more variables, a multiple integral will yield hypervolumes of multi-dimensional functions.

a. Double integral
b. Risch algorithm
c. Constant of integration
d. Trigonometric substitution

36. Integration is an important concept in mathematics, specifically in the field of calculus and, more broadly, mathematical analysis. Given a function f of a real variable x and an interval [a, b] of the real line, the _____

$$\int_a^b f(x)\,dx,$$

is defined informally to be the net signed area of the region in the xy-plane bounded by the graph of f, the x-axis, and the vertical lines x = a and x = b.

The term '_____' may also refer to the notion of antiderivative, a function F whose derivative is the given function f.

a. Integral test for convergence
b. Integrand
c. Indefinite integral
d. Integral

37. The function $\log_b(x)$ depends on both b and x, but the term _____ in standard usage refers to a function of the form $\log_b(x)$ in which the base b is fixed and so the only argument is x. Thus there is one _____ for each value of the base b (which must be positive and must differ from 1.) Viewed in this way, the base-b _____ is the inverse function of the exponential function b^x.

a. 15 theorem
b. BDDC
c. BIBO stability
d. Logarithm function

38. In mathematics, the _____ of a function y = f(x) is a function that, in some fashion, 'undoes' the effect of f The _____ of f is denoted f^{-1}. The statements y=f(x) and x=f^{-1}(y) are equivalent.
    a. ALGOR
    b. Inverse
    c. AUSM
    d. ACTRAN

39. The _____, formerly known as the hyperbolic logarithm, is the logarithm to the base e, where e is an irrational constant approximately equal to 2.718281828. It is also sometimes referred to as the Napierian logarithm, although the original meaning of this term is slightly different. In simple terms, the _____ of a number x is the power to which e would have to be raised to equal x -- for example the natural log of e itself is 1 because e^1 = e, while the _____ of 1 would be 0, since e^0 = 1.
    a. BIBO stability
    b. 15 theorem
    c. BDDC
    d. Natural logarithm

40. The _____ of a quantity whose value decreases with time is the interval required for the quantity to decay to half of its initial value. The concept originated in describing how long it takes atoms to undergo radioactive decay but also applies in a wide variety of other situations.

The term '_____' dates to 1907.

    a. BIBO stability
    b. 15 theorem
    c. BDDC
    d. Half-life

41. The _____ of a material is defined as its mass per unit volume. The symbol of _____ is ρ '>rho.)

Mathematically:

$$d = \frac{m}{V}$$

where:

    d is the _____,
    m is the mass,
    V is the volume.

a. BIBO stability
b. Density
c. 15 theorem
d. BDDC

42. In mathematics, a probability _____ is a function that represents a probability distribution in terms of integrals.

Formally, a probability distribution has density f, if f is a non-negative Lebesgue-integrable function $\mathbb{R} \rightarrow \mathbb{R}$ such that the probability of the interval [a, b] is given by

$$\int_a^b f(x)\,dx$$

for any two numbers a and b. This implies that the total integral of f must be 1.

a. BDDC
b. 15 theorem
c. Density function
d. Factorial moment generating function

43. In mathematics, a (topological) _____ is defined as follows: let I be an interval of real numbers (i.e. a non-empty connected subset of $\mathbb{R}$); then a _____ γ is a continuous mapping $\gamma : I \rightarrow X$, where X is a topological space. The _____ γ is said to be simple if it is injective, i.e. if for all x, y in I, we have $\gamma(x) = \gamma(y) \implies x = y$. If I is a closed bounded interval $[a, b]$, we also allow the possibility $\gamma(a) = \gamma(b)$ (this convention makes it possible to talk about closed simple _____.)

a. Closed curve
b. Tractrix
c. Prolate cycloid
d. Curve

Chapter 3. THE DERIVATIVE

1. In calculus, a branch of mathematics, the _____ is a measurement of how a function changes when its input changes. Loosely speaking, a _____ can be thought of as how much a quantity is changing at some given point. For example, the _____ of the position (or distance) of a vehicle with respect to time is the instantaneous velocity (respectively, instantaneous speed) at which the vehicle is traveling.

The process of finding a _____ is called differentiation. The fundamental theorem of calculus states that differentiation is the reverse process to integration.

   a. Bounded function
   b. Stationary phase approximation
   c. Derivative
   d. Semi-differentiability

2. In mathematics, the concept of a '_____' is used to describe the behavior of a function as its argument or input either 'gets close' to some point, or as the argument becomes arbitrarily large; or the behavior of a sequence's elements as their index increases indefinitely. Limits are used in calculus and other branches of mathematical analysis to define derivatives and continuity.

In formulas, _____ is usually abbreviated as lim

   a. 15 theorem
   b. BDDC
   c. BIBO stability
   d. Limit

3. In calculus, a _____ is either of the two limits of a function f(x) of a real variable x as x approaches a specified point either from below or from above. One should write either:

$$\lim_{x \to a^+} f(x) \text{ or } \lim_{x \downarrow a} f(x)$$

for the limit as x decreases in value approaching a (x approaches a 'from above' or 'from the right'), and similarly

$$\lim_{x \to a^-} f(x) \text{ or } \lim_{x \uparrow a} f(x)$$

for the limit as x increases in value approaching a (x approaches a 'from below' or 'from the left'.)

The two one-sided limits exist and are equal if and only if the limit of f(x) as x approaches a exists.

Chapter 3. THE DERIVATIVE

a. ALGOR
b. ACTRAN
c. AUSM
d. One-sided Limit

4. An _____ of a real-valued function y = f(x) is a curve which describes the behavior of f as either x or y tends to infinity.

In other words, as one moves along the graph of f(x) in some direction, the distance between it and the _____ eventually becomes smaller than any distance that one may specify.

a. ACTRAN
b. Asymptote
c. AUSM
d. ALGOR

5. Suppose f is a function. Then the line y = a is a _____ for f if

$$\lim_{x \to \infty} f(x) = a \quad \text{or} \quad \lim_{x \to -\infty} f(x) = a.$$

Intuitively, this means that f(x) can be made as close as desired to a by making x big enough. How big is big enough depends on how close one wishes to make f(x) to a.

a. Mountain pass theorem
b. Third derivative
c. Second derivative
d. Horizontal asymptote

6. The line x = a is a _____ of a curve y=f(x) if at least one of the following statements is true:

1. $\lim_{x \to a} f(x) = \pm\infty$
2. $\lim_{x \to a^-} f(x) = \pm\infty$
3. $\lim_{x \to a^+} f(x) = \pm\infty$

Intuitively, if x = a is an asymptote of f, then, if we imagine x approaching a from one side, the value of f(x) grows without bound; i.e., f(x) becomes large (positively or negatively), and, in fact, becomes larger than any finite value.

Note that f(x) may or may not be defined at a: what the function is doing precisely at x = a does not affect the asymptote. For example, consider the function

$$f(x) = \begin{cases} \frac{1}{x} & \text{if } x > 0, \\ 5 & \text{if } x \leq 0 \end{cases}$$

As $\lim_{x \to 0^+} f(x) = \infty$, f(x) has a _____ at 0, even though f(0) = 5.

Another example is $f(x) = 1/(x-1)$ which has a _____ of x=1 as shown by the limit

$$\lim_{x \to 1^+} \frac{1}{x-1} = \infty$$

In the graph of $f(x) = x + \frac{1}{x}$, the y-axis (x = 0) and the line y = x are both asymptotes.

When a linear asymptote is not parallel to the x- or y-axis, it is called either an oblique asymptote or equivalently a slant asymptote.

a. Ramp function
b. Third derivative
c. Monodromy
d. Vertical asymptote

7. Continuous functions are of utmost importance in mathematics and applications. However, not all functions are continuous. If a function is not continuous at a point in its domain, one says that it has a _____ there. The set of all points of _____ of a function may be a discrete set, a dense set, or even the entire domain of the function.
   a. BDDC
   b. 15 theorem
   c. Vector
   d. Discontinuity

8. In calculus, an _____, primitive or indefinite integral of a function f is a function F whose derivative is equal to f, i.e., F >' = f. The process of solving for antiderivatives is antidifferentiation (or indefinite integration.) Antiderivatives are related to definite integrals through the fundamental theorem of calculus: the definite integral of a function over an interval is equal to the difference between the values of an _____ evaluated at the endpoints of the interval.

a. Order of integration
b. Antiderivative
c. Indefinite integral
d. Integrand

9. In mathematics, a _____ is a function for which, intuitively, small changes in the input result in small changes in the output. Otherwise, a function is said to be discontinuous. A _____ with a continuous inverse function is called bicontinuous. An intuitive though imprecise (and inexact) idea of continuity is given by the common statement that a _____ is a function whose graph can be drawn without lifting the chalk from the blackboard.

a. Visual Calculus
b. Binomial series
c. Hyperbolic angle
d. Continuous Function

10. In mathematics, a _____ is a function whose definition is dependent on the value of the independent variable. Mathematically, a real-valued function f of a real variable x is a relationship whose definition is given differently on disjoint subsets of its domain

The word piecewise is also used to describe any property of a _____ that holds for each piece but may not hold for the whole domain of the function.

a. Piecewise-defined function
b. Range
c. Surjective
d. Constant function

11. The _____ is a function in mathematics. The application of this function to a value x is written as exp(x). Equivalently, this can be written in the form e^x, where e is a mathematical constant, the base of the natural logarithm, which equals approximately 2.718281828, and is also known as Euler's number.

a. Integral part
b. Area hyperbolic functions
c. ACTRAN
d. Exponential function

12. The function $\log_b(x)$ depends on both b and x, but the term _____ in standard usage refers to a function of the form $\log_b(x)$ in which the base b is fixed and so the only argument is x. Thus there is one _____ for each value of the base b (which must be positive and must differ from 1.) Viewed in this way, the base-b _____ is the inverse function of the exponential function b^x.

a. Logarithm function
b. BDDC
c. BIBO stability
d. 15 theorem

13. In mathematics, a _____ is any function which can be written as the ratio of two polynomial functions.

$$y = \frac{x^2 - 3x - 2}{x^2 - 4}$$

In the case of one variable, x, a _____ is a function of the form

$$f(x) = \frac{P(x)}{Q(x)}$$

where P and Q are polynomial function in x and Q is not the zero polynomial. The domain of f is the set of all points x for which the denominator Q(x) is not zero.

a. BIBO stability
b. 15 theorem
c. Rational function
d. BDDC

14. _____ is the concept of adding accumulated interest back to the principal, so that interest is earned on interest from that moment on. The act of declaring interest to be principal is called compounding (i.e., interest is compounded.) A loan, for example, may have its interest compounded every month: in this case, a loan with $100 principal and 1% interest per month would have a balance of $101 at the end of the first month.

a. BIBO stability
b. BDDC
c. 15 theorem
d. Compound interest

Chapter 3. THE DERIVATIVE

15. In mathematical analysis, the _____ states that for each value between the least upper bound and greatest lower bound of the image of a continuous function there is a corresponding value in its domain mapping to the original. _____

- Version I. The _____ states the following: If the function y = f(x) is continuous on the interval [a, b], and u is a number between f(a) and f(b), then there is a c ∈ [a, b] such that f(c) = u.

- Version II. Suppose that I is an interval [a, b] in the real numbers R and that f : I → R is a continuous function. Then the image set f(I) is also an interval, and either it contains [f(a), f(b)], or it contains [f(b), f(a)]; that is,

    f(I) ⊇ [f(a), f(b)], or f(I) ⊇ [f(b), f(a)].

It is frequently stated in the following equivalent form: Suppose that f : [a, b] → R is continuous and that u is a real number satisfying f(a) < u < f(b) or f(a) > u > f(b.) Then for some c ∈ [a, b], f(c) = u.

This captures an intuitive property of continuous functions: given f continuous on [1, 2], if f(1) = 3 and f(2) = 5 then f must take the value 4 somewhere between 1 and 2.

a. ACTRAN
b. ALGOR
c. Intermediate Value Theorem
d. AUSM

16. The function difference divided by the point difference is known as the _____, it is also known as Newton's quotient):

$$\frac{\Delta F(P)}{\Delta P} = \frac{F(P + \Delta P) - F(P)}{\Delta P} = \frac{\nabla F(P + \Delta P)}{\Delta P}.$$

If ΔP is infinitesimal, then the _____ is a derivative, otherwise it is a divided difference:

$$\text{If } |\Delta P| = \iota ota: \quad \frac{\Delta F(P)}{\Delta P} = \frac{dF(P)}{dP} = F'(P) = G(P);$$

$$\text{If } |\Delta P| > \iota ota: \quad \frac{\Delta F(P)}{\Delta P} = \frac{DF(P)}{DP} = F[P, P + \Delta P].$$

Chapter 3. THE DERIVATIVE

Regardless if ΔP is infinitesimal or finite, there is (at least--in the case of the derivative--theoretically) a point range, where the boundaries are $P \pm (.5)\Delta P$ (depending on the orientation--$\Delta F(P)$, $\delta F(P)$ or $\nabla F(P)$):

　　　　LB = Lower Boundary; UB = Upper Boundary;

Anyone familiar with derivatives knows that they can be regarded as functions themselves, harboring their own derivatives. Thus each function is home to sequential degrees ('higher orders') of derivation, or differentiation. This property can be generalized to all difference quotients. As this sequencing requires a corresponding boundary splintering, it is practical to break up the point range into smaller, equi-sized sections, with each section being marked by an intermediary point ('P_i''), where LB = P_0 and UB = P_{A_n}, the nth point, equaling the degree/order:

LB = $P_0 = P_0 + 0\Delta_1 P = P_{A_n} - (\mathring{A}f - 0)\Delta_1 P$; $P_1 = P_0 + 1\Delta_1 P = P_{A_n} - (\mathring{A}f - 1)\Delta_1 P$; $P_2 = P_0 + 2\Delta_1 P = P_{A_n} - (\mathring{A}f - 2)\Delta_1 P$; $P_3 = P_0 + 3\Delta_1 P = P_{A_n} - (\mathring{A}f - 3)\Delta_1 P$; ↓↓↓↓ $P_{A_n - 3} = P_0 + (\mathring{A}f - 3)\Delta_1 P = P_{A_n} - 3\Delta_1 P$; $P_{A_n - 2} = P_0 + (\mathring{A}f - 2)\Delta_1 P = P_{A_n} - 2\Delta_1 P$; $P_{A_n - 1} = P_0 + (\mathring{A}f - 1)\Delta_1 P = P_{A_n} - 1\Delta_1 P$; UB = $P_{A_n - 0} = P_0 + (\mathring{A}f - 0)\Delta_1 P = P_{A_n} - 0\Delta_1 P = P_{A_n}$;

$\Delta P = \Delta_1 P = P_1 - P_0 = P_2 - P_1 = P_3 - P_2 = \ldots$

　　a. Directional derivative
　　b. Notation for differentiation
　　c. Continuously differentiable
　　d. Difference quotient

17. _____ is used to describe the steepness, incline, gradient, or grade of a straight line. A higher _____ value indicates a steeper incline. The _____ is defined as the ratio of the 'rise' divided by the 'run' between two points on a line, or in other words, the ratio of the altitude change to the horizontal distance between any two points on the line.
　　a. 15 theorem
　　b. Sequence
　　c. Y-intercept
　　d. Slope

18. A _____ of a curve is a line that (locally) intersects two points on the curve. The word secant comes from the Latin secare, for to cut.

It can be used to approximate the tangent to a curve, at some point P. If the secant to a curve is defined by two points, P and Q, with P fixed and Q variable, as Q approaches P along the curve, the direction of the secant approaches that of the tangent at P, assuming there is just one.

Chapter 3. THE DERIVATIVE

a. Witch of Agnesi
b. Curve
c. Kappa curve
d. Secant line

19. In geometry, the _____ (or simply the tangent) to a curve at a given point is the straight line that 'just touches' the curve at that point (in the sense explained more precisely below.) As it passes through the point of tangency, the _____ is 'going in the same direction' as the curve, and in this sense it is the best straight-line approximation to the curve at that point. The same definition applies to space curves and curves in n-dimensional Euclidean space.
   a. Minimal surface
   b. North pole
   c. Lie derivative
   d. Tangent line

20. Trigonometry is a branch of mathematics that deals with triangles, particularly those plane triangles in which one angle has 90 degrees (right triangles.) Trigonometry deals with relationships between the sides and the angles of triangles and with the _____ functions, which describe those relationships.

Trigonometry has applications in both pure mathematics and in applied mathematics, where it is essential in many branches of science and technology.

   a. Trigonometric functions
   b. Sine
   c. Trigonometric integrals
   d. Trigonometric

21. In mathematics, the _____ are functions of an angle. They are important in the study of triangles and modeling periodic phenomena, among many other applications. _____ are commonly defined as ratios of two sides of a right triangle containing the angle, and can equivalently be defined as the lengths of various line segments from a unit circle.
   a. Sine integral
   b. Trigonometric
   c. Trigonometric integrals
   d. Trigonometric functions

Chapter 3. THE DERIVATIVE

22. In mathematics, a (topological) _____ is defined as follows: let I be an interval of real numbers (i.e. a non-empty connected subset of $\mathbb{R}$); then a _____ γ is a continuous mapping $\gamma : I \to X$, where X is a topological space. The _____ γ is said to be simple if it is injective, i.e. if for all x, y in I, we have $\gamma(x) = \gamma(y) \implies x = y$. If I is a closed bounded interval $[a, b]$, we also allow the possibility $\gamma(a) = \gamma(b)$ (this convention makes it possible to talk about closed simple _____.)

   a. Closed curve
   b. Tractrix
   c. Prolate cycloid
   d. Curve

23. In infinitesimal calculus, a _____ is traditionally an infinitesimally small change in a variable. For example, if x is a variable, then a change in the value of x is often denoted Δx (or δx when this change is considered to be small.) The _____ dx represents such a change, but is infinitely small.

   a. The Method of Mechanical Theorems
   b. Local maximum
   c. Dirichlet integral
   d. Differential

24. A _____ is a mathematical equation for an unknown function of one or several variables that relates the values of the function itself and of its derivatives of various orders. they play a prominent role in engineering, physics, economics and other disciplines.

   A simplified real world example of a _____ is modeling the acceleration of a ball falling through the air (considering only gravity and air resistance.)

   a. Caloric polynomial
   b. Differential equation
   c. Phase line
   d. Structural stability

25. In mathematics, the _____ (or modulus) of a real number is its numerical value without regard to its sign. So, for example, 3 is the _____ of both 3 and −3.

   The _____ of a number a is denoted by $|a|$.

a. ACTRAN
b. Area hyperbolic functions
c. Exponential function
d. Absolute value

Chapter 4. CALCULATING THE DERIVATIVE

1. _____ is a type of motion in which the velocity of an object changes equal amounts in equal time periods. An example of an object having _____ would be a ball rolling down a ramp. The object picks up velocity as it goes down the ramp with equal changes in time.
   a. Uniform Acceleration
   b. AUSM
   c. ALGOR
   d. ACTRAN

2. In calculus, a branch of mathematics, the _____ is a measurement of how a function changes when its input changes. Loosely speaking, a _____ can be thought of as how much a quantity is changing at some given point. For example, the _____ of the position (or distance) of a vehicle with respect to time is the instantaneous velocity (respectively, instantaneous speed) at which the vehicle is traveling.

   The process of finding a _____ is called differentiation. The fundamental theorem of calculus states that differentiation is the reverse process to integration.

   a. Semi-differentiability
   b. Derivative
   c. Stationary phase approximation
   d. Bounded function

3. In calculus, _____, was originally the use of expressions such as dx and dy and to represent 'infinitely small' (or infinitesimal) increments of quantities x and y, just as >Δx and >Δy represent finite increments of x and y respectively. So for y being a function of x, or

   [image]>

the derivative of y with respect to x, which later came to be viewed as

   [image]>

was, according to Leibniz, the quotient of an infinitesimal increment of y by an infinitesimal increment of x, or

   [image]>

where the right hand side is Lagrange's notation for the derivative of f at x.

Similarly, although mathematicians usually now view an integral

as a limit

where >Δx is an interval containing x_i, Leibniz viewed it as the sum (the integral sign denoting summation) of infinitely many infinitesimal quantities f(x) dx.

a. Leibniz's notation
b. Stationary point
c. Time derivative
d. Smooth function

4. In calculus, an _____, primitive or indefinite integral of a function f is a function F whose derivative is equal to f, i.e., F >' = f. The process of solving for antiderivatives is antidifferentiation (or indefinite integration.) Antiderivatives are related to definite integrals through the fundamental theorem of calculus: the definite integral of a function over an interval is equal to the difference between the values of an _____ evaluated at the endpoints of the interval.

a. Order of integration
b. Integrand
c. Indefinite integral
d. Antiderivative

Chapter 4. CALCULATING THE DERIVATIVE

5. In elementary algebra, a _____ is a polynomial with two terms--the sum of two monomials--often bound by parenthesis or brackets when operated upon. It is the simplest kind of polynomial other than monomials.

- The _____ $a^2 - b^2$ can be factored as the product of two other binomials:

    $a^2 - b^2 = (a + b)(a - b.)$

    This is a special case of the more general formula:

    $$a^{n+1} - b^{n+1} = (a - b) \sum_{k=0}^{n} a^k b^{n-k}.$$

- The product of a pair of linear binomials (ax + b) and (cx + d) is:

    $(ax + b)(cx + d) = acx^2 + axd + bcx + bd.$

- A _____ raised to the nth power, represented as

    $(a + b)^n$

    can be expanded by means of the _____ theorem or, equivalently, using Pascal's triangle. Taking a simple example, the perfect square _____ $(p + q)^2$ can be found by squaring the first digit, adding twice the product of the first and second digit and finally adding the square of the second digit, to give $p^2 + 2pq + q^2$.

a. Partial fractions
b. Multinomial theorem
c. Completing the square
d. Binomial

6. In mathematics, the _____ is an important formula giving the expansion of powers of sums. Its simplest version states that

$$(x + y)^n = \sum_{k=0}^{n} \binom{n}{k} x^{n-k} y^k \qquad (1)$$

for any real or complex numbers x and y, and any non-negative integer n. The binomial coefficient appearing in (1) may be defined in terms of the factorial function n!:

$$\binom{n}{k} = \frac{n!}{k!\,(n-k)!}.$$

For example, here are the cases where 2 ≤ n ≤ 5:

$$(x+y)^2 = x^2 + 2xy + y^2$$
$$(x+y)^3 = x^3 + 3x^2y + 3xy^2 + y^3$$
$$(x+y)^4 = x^4 + 4x^3y + 6x^2y^2 + 4xy^3 + y^4$$
$$(x+y)^5 = x^5 + 5x^4y + 10x^3y^2 + 10x^2y^3 + 5xy^4 + y^5.$$

Formula (1) is valid more generally for any elements x and y of a semiring as long as xy = yx.

a. Central binomial coefficient
b. Hypergeometric identities
c. Trinomial expansion
d. Binomial theorem

7. This article will state and prove the _____ for differentiation, and then use it to prove these two formulas.

The _____ for differentiation states that for every natural number n, the derivative of $f(x) = x^n$ is $f'(x) = nx^{n-1}$, that is,

$$(x^n)' = nx^{n-1}.$$

The _____ for integration

$$\int x^n \, dx = \frac{x^{n+1}}{n+1} + C$$

for natural n is then an easy consequence. One just needs to take the derivative of this equality and use the _____ and linearity of differentiation on the right-hand side.

a. Power rule
b. Functional integration
c. Leibniz rule
d. Test for Divergence

8. In calculus, the _____ is a formula used to find the derivatives of products of functions. It may be stated thus:

$$(f \cdot g)' = f' \cdot g + f \cdot g'$$

or in the Leibniz notation thus:

$$\frac{d}{dx}(u \cdot v) = u \cdot \frac{dv}{dx} + v \cdot \frac{du}{dx}.$$

Discovery of this rule is credited to Gottfried Leibniz, who demonstrated it using differentials. Here is Leibniz's argument: Let u and v be two differentiable functions of x.

a. Quotient Rule
b. Constant factor rule in differentiation
c. Differentiation rules
d. Product rule

9. In calculus, the _____ is a method of finding the derivative of a function that is the quotient of two other functions for which derivatives exist.

If the function one wishes to differentiate, f(x), can be written as

$$f(x) = \frac{g(x)}{h(x)}$$

and h(x) ≠ 0, then the rule states that the derivative of g(x) / h(x) is equal to:

$$\frac{d}{dx}f(x) = f'(x) = \frac{g'(x)h(x) - g(x)h'(x)}{[h(x)]^2}.$$

Or, more precisely, if all x in some open set containing the number a satisfy h(x) ≠ 0; and g'(a) and h'(a) both exist; then, f'(a) exists as well and:

$$f'(a) = \frac{g'(a)h(a) - g(a)h'(a)}{[h(a)]^2}.$$

Chapter 4. CALCULATING THE DERIVATIVE

The derivative of $(4x - 2) / (x^2 + 1)$ is:

$$\frac{d}{dx}\left[\frac{(4x-2)}{x^2+1}\right] = \frac{(x^2+1)(4) - (4x-2)(2x)}{(x^2+1)^2}$$

$$= \frac{(4x^2+4) - (8x^2-4x)}{(x^2+1)^2} = \frac{-4x^2+4x+4}{(x^2+1)^2}$$

In the example above, the choices

$g(x) = 4x - 2$
$h(x) = x^2 + 1$

were made. Analogously, the derivative of $\sin(x) / x^2$ (when $x \neq 0$) is:

$$\frac{\cos(x)x^2 - \sin(x)2x}{x^4}$$

Another example is:

$$f(x) = \frac{2x^2}{x^3}$$

whereas $g(x) = 2x^2$ and $h(x) = x^3$, and $g'(x) = 4x$ and $h'(x) = 3x^2$.

a. Constant factor rule in differentiation
b. Differentiation rules
c. Reciprocal Rule
d. Quotient rule

10. In economics, _____ is equal to total cost divided by the number of goods produced (the output quantity, Q.) It is also equal to the sum of average variable costs (total variable costs divided by Q) plus average fixed costs (total fixed costs divided by Q.) Average costs may be dependent on the time period considered (increasing production may be expensive or impossible in the short term, for example.)
a. AUSM
b. ALGOR
c. ACTRAN
d. Average cost

Chapter 4. CALCULATING THE DERIVATIVE

11. In a totally ordered set all elements are mutually comparable, so such a set can have at most one minimal element and at most one maximal element. Then, due to mutual comparability, the minimal element will also be the least element and the maximal element will also be the greatest element. Thus in a totally ordered set we can simply use the terms _____ and maximum.
    a. Ghosts of departed quantities
    b. Maximum
    c. Minimum
    d. Nth term

12. In a totally ordered set all elements are mutually comparable, so such a set can have at most one minimal element and at most one maximal element. Then, due to mutual comparability, the minimal element will also be the least element and the maximal element will also be the greatest element. Thus in a totally ordered set we can simply use the terms minimum and _____.
    a. Maximum
    b. Racetrack principle
    c. Leibniz rule
    d. Nth term

13. In calculus, the _____ is a formula for the derivative of the composite of two functions.

    In intuitive terms, if a variable, y, depends on a second variable, u, which in turn depends on a third variable, x, then the rate of change of y with respect to x can be computed as the rate of change of y with respect to u multiplied by the rate of change of u with respect to x. Schematically,

    $$\frac{dy}{dx} = \frac{dy}{du} \cdot \frac{du}{dx}.$$

    a. Differentiation rules
    b. Product rule
    c. Reciprocal Rule
    d. Chain rule

14. In mathematics, a _____ represents the application of one function to the results of another. For instance, the functions f: X → Y and g: Y → Z can be composed by first computing f(x) and then applying a function g to the output of f(x.)

    Thus one obtains a function g ∘ f: X → Z defined by (g ∘ f)(x) = g(f(x)) for all x in X. The notation g ∘ f is read as 'g circle f', or 'g composed with f', 'g after f', 'g following f', or just 'g of f'.

Chapter 4. CALCULATING THE DERIVATIVE

a. Surjective
b. Piecewise-defined function
c. Constant function
d. Composite function

15. The _____ is a function in mathematics. The application of this function to a value x is written as exp(x). Equivalently, this can be written in the form e^x, where e is a mathematical constant, the base of the natural logarithm, which equals approximately 2.718281828, and is also known as Euler's number.
   a. Integral part
   b. Area hyperbolic functions
   c. ACTRAN
   d. Exponential function

16. _____ is the concept of adding accumulated interest back to the principal, so that interest is earned on interest from that moment on. The act of declaring interest to be principal is called compounding (i.e., interest is compounded.) A loan, for example, may have its interest compounded every month: in this case, a loan with $100 principal and 1% interest per month would have a balance of $101 at the end of the first month.
   a. BDDC
   b. BIBO stability
   c. 15 theorem
   d. Compound interest

17. A _____ or logistic curve is the most common sigmoid curve. It models the S-curve of growth of some set P, where P might be thought of as population. The initial stage of growth is approximately exponential; then, as saturation begins, the growth slows, and at maturity, growth stops.
   a. 15 theorem
   b. Logarithmic integral function
   c. Multiplication theorem
   d. Logistic function

18. The function $\log_b(x)$ depends on both b and x, but the term _____ in standard usage refers to a function of the form $\log_b(x)$ in which the base b is fixed and so the only argument is x. Thus there is one _____ for each value of the base b (which must be positive and must differ from 1.) Viewed in this way, the base-b _____ is the inverse function of the exponential function b^x.

a. 15 theorem
b. BDDC
c. BIBO stability
d. Logarithm function

19. In mathematics, a _____ is a function whose values do not vary and thus are constant. For example, if we have the function f(x) = 4, then f is constant since f maps any value to 4. More formally, a function f : A → B is a _____ if f(x) = f(y) for all x and y in A.
    a. Constant function
    b. Range
    c. Piecewise-defined function
    d. Surjective

Chapter 5. GRAPHS AND THE DERIVATIVE

1. Let f be a differentiable function, and let f'(x) be its derivative. The derivative of f'(x) (if it has one) is written f''(x) and is called the _____ of f. Similarly, the derivative of a _____, if it exists, is written f'''(x) and is called the third derivative of f.

    a. Slant asymptote
    b. Second derivative
    c. Stationary phase approximation
    d. Vertical asymptote

2. In calculus, a branch of mathematics, the _____ is a measurement of how a function changes when its input changes. Loosely speaking, a _____ can be thought of as how much a quantity is changing at some given point. For example, the _____ of the position (or distance) of a vehicle with respect to time is the instantaneous velocity (respectively, instantaneous speed) at which the vehicle is traveling.

   The process of finding a _____ is called differentiation. The fundamental theorem of calculus states that differentiation is the reverse process to integration.

    a. Stationary phase approximation
    b. Bounded function
    c. Semi-differentiability
    d. Derivative

3. In mathematics, a _____ is a function which preserves the given order. This concept first arose in calculus, and was later generalized to the more abstract setting of order theory.

   In calculus, a function f defined on a subset of the real numbers with real values is called monotonic (also monotonically increasing or non-decreasing), if for all x and y such that x >≤ y one has f(x) >≤ f(y), so f preserves the order.

    a. Pettis integral
    b. 15 theorem
    c. Monotonic function
    d. Pseudo-differential operator

4. In calculus, an _____, primitive or indefinite integral of a function f is a function F whose derivative is equal to f, i.e., F >' = f. The process of solving for antiderivatives is antidifferentiation (or indefinite integration.) Antiderivatives are related to definite integrals through the fundamental theorem of calculus: the definite integral of a function over an interval is equal to the difference between the values of an _____ evaluated at the endpoints of the interval.

Chapter 5. GRAPHS AND THE DERIVATIVE

a. Integrand
b. Order of integration
c. Indefinite integral
d. Antiderivative

5. In mathematics, a _____ (or critical number) is a point on the domain of a function where:

- one dimension: the derivative (or slope of the line when visualized) is equal to zero or a point where the function ceases to be differentiable.
- in general: there are two distinct concepts: either the derivative (Jacobian) vanishes, or it is not of full rank (or, in either case, the function is not differentiable); these agree in one dimension.

Note that in one dimension, a critical value or critical number x of function f is the domain element at which the derivative is zero or undefined, whereas the associated ordered pair (x, y) is the _____. In higher dimensions a critical value is in the range whereas a _____ is in the domain.

There are two situations in which a point becomes a _____ of a function of one variable. The first of which is that the value of the first derivative is equal to zero.

a. Differentiation operator
b. Critical point
c. Total derivative
d. Multivariable calculus

6. Trigonometry is a branch of mathematics that deals with triangles, particularly those plane triangles in which one angle has 90 degrees (right triangles.) Trigonometry deals with relationships between the sides and the angles of triangles and with the _____ functions, which describe those relationships.

Trigonometry has applications in both pure mathematics and in applied mathematics, where it is essential in many branches of science and technology.

a. Trigonometric integrals
b. Trigonometric
c. Sine
d. Trigonometric functions

7. In mathematics, the _____ are functions of an angle. They are important in the study of triangles and modeling periodic phenomena, among many other applications. _____ are commonly defined as ratios of two sides of a right triangle containing the angle, and can equivalently be defined as the lengths of various line segments from a unit circle.

a. Trigonometric integrals
b. Sine integral
c. Trigonometric
d. Trigonometric functions

8. In mathematics, _____ and minima, known collectively as extrema, are the largest value (maximum) or smallest value (minimum), that a function takes in a point either within a given neighbourhood (local extremum) or on the function domain in its entirety (global extremum.)

Throughout, a point refers to an input (x), while a value refers to an output (y): one distinguishing between the maximum value and the point (or points) at which it occurs.

A real-valued function f defined on the real line is said to have a local maximum point at the point x^*, if there exists some $\varepsilon > 0$, such that $f(x^*) \geq f(x)$ when $|x - x^*| < \varepsilon$.

a. Leibniz formula
b. Racetrack principle
c. Maxima
d. Related rates

9. In a totally ordered set all elements are mutually comparable, so such a set can have at most one minimal element and at most one maximal element. Then, due to mutual comparability, the minimal element will also be the least element and the maximal element will also be the greatest element. Thus in a totally ordered set we can simply use the terms minimum and _____.

a. Maximum
b. Nth term
c. Racetrack principle
d. Leibniz rule

10. In a totally ordered set all elements are mutually comparable, so such a set can have at most one minimal element and at most one maximal element. Then, due to mutual comparability, the minimal element will also be the least element and the maximal element will also be the greatest element. Thus in a totally ordered set we can simply use the terms _____ and maximum.

a. Maximum
b. Ghosts of departed quantities
c. Nth term
d. Minimum

Chapter 5. GRAPHS AND THE DERIVATIVE

11. In calculus, the _____ determines whether a given critical point of a function is a maximum, a minimum, or neither.

Suppose that f is a function and we want to determine if f has a maximum or minimum at x. If f is increasing to the left of x and decreasing to the right of x, then x is a local maximum of f.

   a. Continuous function
   b. Partial sum
   c. Test for Divergence
   d. First derivative test

12. In mathematics, a _____ is a polynomial equation of the second degree. The general form is

$$ax^2 + bx + c = 0,$$

where a ≠ 0.

Students and teachers all over the world are familiar with the quadratic formula that can be derived by completing the square.

   a. Stern-Brocot tree
   b. Quadratic equation
   c. Lochs' theorem
   d. Continued fraction

13. A quadratic equation with real or complex coefficients has two solutions (or roots), not necessarily distinct, which may or may not be real, given by the _____:

$$\frac{-b \pm \sqrt{b^2 - 4ac}}{2a}$$

Example discriminant signsâ— <0: $x^2+\frac{1}{2}$â— =0: $-\frac{4}{3}x^2+\frac{4}{3}x-\frac{1}{3}$â— >0: $\frac{3}{2}x^2+\frac{1}{2}x-\frac{4}{3}$

In the above formula, the expression underneath the square root sign

$$D = b^2 - 4ac,$$

is called the discriminant of the quadratic equation.

Chapter 5. GRAPHS AND THE DERIVATIVE

A quadratic equation with real coefficients can have either one or two distinct real roots, or two distinct complex roots. In this case the discriminant determines the number and nature of the roots.

a. Cubic function
b. Quartic function
c. Linear equation
d. Quadratic formula

14. In mathematics, the _____ (or replacement set) of a given function is the set of 'input' values for which the function is defined. For instance, the _____ of cosine would be all real numbers, while the _____ of the square root would be only numbers greater than or equal to 0 (ignoring complex numbers in both cases.) In a representation of a function in a xy Cartesian coordinate system, the _____ is represented on the x axis (or abscissa.)

a. Domain
b. BDDC
c. 15 theorem
d. BIBO stability

15. Let f be a differentiable function, and let f'(x) be its derivative. The derivative of f'(x) (if it has one) is written f''(x) and is called the second derivative of f. Similarly, the derivative of a second derivative, if it exists, is written f'''(x) and is called the _____ of f.

a. Differential coefficient
b. Mountain pass theorem
c. Third derivative
d. Derivative

16. In calculus, the _____ is a formula used to find the derivatives of products of functions. It may be stated thus:

$$(f \cdot g)' = f' \cdot g + f \cdot g'$$

or in the Leibniz notation thus:

$$\frac{d}{dx}(u \cdot v) = u \cdot \frac{dv}{dx} + v \cdot \frac{du}{dx}.$$

Discovery of this rule is credited to Gottfried Leibniz, who demonstrated it using differentials. Here is Leibniz's argument: Let u and v be two differentiable functions of x.

Chapter 5. GRAPHS AND THE DERIVATIVE

a. Quotient Rule
b. Constant factor rule in differentiation
c. Product rule
d. Differentiation rules

17. In physics, and more specifically kinematics, _____ is the change in velocity over time. Because velocity is a vector, it can change in two ways: a change in magnitude and/or a change in direction. In one dimension, _____ is the rate at which something speeds up or slows down.

a. ALGOR
b. ACTRAN
c. Acceleration
d. AUSM

18. In calculus, the _____ is a method of finding the derivative of a function that is the quotient of two other functions for which derivatives exist.

If the function one wishes to differentiate, f(x), can be written as

$$f(x) = \frac{g(x)}{h(x)}$$

and h(x) ≠ 0, then the rule states that the derivative of g(x) / h(x) is equal to:

$$\frac{d}{dx}f(x) = f'(x) = \frac{g'(x)h(x) - g(x)h'(x)}{[h(x)]^2}.$$

Or, more precisely, if all x in some open set containing the number a satisfy h(x) ≠ 0; and g'(a) and h'(a) both exist; then, f'(a) exists as well and:

$$f'(a) = \frac{g'(a)h(a) - g(a)h'(a)}{[h(a)]^2}.$$

Chapter 5. GRAPHS AND THE DERIVATIVE

The derivative of (4x − 2) / (x² + 1) is:

$$\frac{d}{dx}\left[\frac{(4x-2)}{x^2+1}\right] = \frac{(x^2+1)(4)-(4x-2)(2x)}{(x^2+1)^2}$$

$$= \frac{(4x^2+4)-(8x^2-4x)}{(x^2+1)^2} = \frac{-4x^2+4x+4}{(x^2+1)^2}$$

In the example above, the choices

g(x) = 4x − 2
h(x) = x² + 1

were made. Analogously, the derivative of sin(x) / x² (when x ≠ 0) is:

$$\frac{\cos(x)x^2 - \sin(x)2x}{x^4}$$

Another example is:

$$f(x) = \frac{2x^2}{x^3}$$

whereas g(x) = 2x² and h(x) = x³, and g'(x) = 4x and h'(x) = 3x².

a. Quotient rule
b. Differentiation rules
c. Constant factor rule in differentiation
d. Reciprocal Rule

19. In physics, _____ is defined as the rate of change of position. it is vector physical quantity; both speed and direction are required to define it. In the SI (metric) system, it is measured in meters per second: (m/s) or ms⁻¹.
a. Velocity
b. BDDC
c. BIBO stability
d. 15 theorem

Chapter 5. GRAPHS AND THE DERIVATIVE

20. In mathematics, a concave function is the negative of a convex function. A concave function is also synonymously called _____, concave down, convex cap or upper convex.

Formally, a real-valued function f defined on an interval (or on any convex set C of some vector space) is called concave, if for any two points x and y in its domain C and any t in [0,1], we have

$$f(tx + (1-t)y) \geq tf(x) + (1-t)f(y).$$

Also, f(x) is concave on [a, b] if and only if the function −f(x) is convex on [a, b].

a. Stationary phase approximation
b. Concave upwards
c. Ramp function
d. Concave downwards

21. In mathematics, a real-valued function f defined on an interval (or on any convex subset of some vector space) is called convex, _____, concave up or convex cup, if for any two points x and y in its domain C and any t in [0,1], we have

$$f(tx + (1-t)y) \leq tf(x) + (1-t)f(y).$$

Convex function on an interval.

In other words, a function is convex if and only if its epigraph (the set of points lying on or above the graph) is a convex set.

Pictorially, a function is called 'convex' if the function lies below the straight line segment connecting two points, for any two points in the interval.

A function is called strictly convex if

$$f(tx + (1-t)y) < tf(x) + (1-t)f(y)$$

for any t in (0,1) and $x \neq y$.

A function f is said to be concave if − f is convex.

a. Mountain pass theorem
b. Vertical asymptote
c. Third derivative
d. Concave upwards

Chapter 5. GRAPHS AND THE DERIVATIVE

22. In differential calculus, an inflection point, or _____ (or inflexion) is a point on a curve at which the curvature changes sign. The curve changes from being concave upwards (positive curvature) to concave downwards (negative curvature), or vice versa. If one imagines driving a vehicle along the curve, it is a point at which the steering-wheel is momentarily 'straight', being turned from left to right or vice versa.
    a. Lin-Tsien equation
    b. Derivative of a constant
    c. Logarithmic derivative
    d. Point of inflection

23. _____ is used to describe the steepness, incline, gradient, or grade of a straight line. A higher _____ value indicates a steeper incline. The _____ is defined as the ratio of the 'rise' divided by the 'run' between two points on a line, or in other words, the ratio of the altitude change to the horizontal distance between any two points on the line.
    a. Slope
    b. 15 theorem
    c. Y-intercept
    d. Sequence

24. In geometry, the _____ (or simply the tangent) to a curve at a given point is the straight line that 'just touches' the curve at that point (in the sense explained more precisely below.) As it passes through the point of tangency, the _____ is 'going in the same direction' as the curve, and in this sense it is the best straight-line approximation to the curve at that point. The same definition applies to space curves and curves in n-dimensional Euclidean space.
    a. Lie derivative
    b. Minimal surface
    c. North pole
    d. Tangent line

25. In calculus, a branch of mathematics, the _____ is a criterion often useful for determining whether a given stationary point of a function is a local maximum or a local minimum.

The test states: If the function f is twice differentiable at a stationary point x, meaning that $f'(x) = 0$, then:

- If $f''(x) < 0$ then f has a local maximum at x.
- If $f''(x) > 0$ then f has a local minimum at x.
- If $f''(x) = 0$, the _____ says nothing about the point x, has a possible inflection point.

In the last case, the function may have a local maximum or minimum there, but the function is sufficiently 'flat' that this is undetected by the second derivative. In this case one has to examine the third derivative. Such an example is f(x) = x^4.

Chapter 5. GRAPHS AND THE DERIVATIVE

a. Symmetric derivative
b. Stationary point
c. Linearity of differentiation
d. Second derivative test

26. In mathematics, a (topological) _____ is defined as follows: let I be an interval of real numbers (i.e. a non-empty connected subset of $\mathbb{R}$); then a _____ γ is a continuous mapping $\gamma : I \to X$, where X is a topological space. The _____ γ is said to be simple if it is injective, i.e. if for all x, y in I, we have $\gamma(x) = \gamma(y) \implies x = y$. If I is a closed bounded interval $[a, b]$, we also allow the possibility $\gamma(a) = \gamma(b)$ (this convention makes it possible to talk about closed simple _____ .)

a. Prolate cycloid
b. Closed curve
c. Tractrix
d. Curve

27. In mathematics, a _____ is any function which can be written as the ratio of two polynomial functions.

$$y = \frac{x^2 - 3x - 2}{x^2 - 4}$$

In the case of one variable, x, a _____ is a function of the form

$$f(x) = \frac{P(x)}{Q(x)}$$

where P and Q are polynomial function in x and Q is not the zero polynomial. The domain of f is the set of all points x for which the denominator Q(x) is not zero.

a. BIBO stability
b. 15 theorem
c. BDDC
d. Rational function

28. An _____ of a real-valued function y = f(x) is a curve which describes the behavior of f as either x or y tends to infinity.

In other words, as one moves along the graph of f(x) in some direction, the distance between it and the _____ eventually becomes smaller than any distance that one may specify.

a. AUSM
b. ALGOR
c. ACTRAN
d. Asymptote

29. Suppose f is a function. Then the line y = a is a _____ for f if

$$\lim_{x \to \infty} f(x) = a \text{ or } \lim_{x \to -\infty} f(x) = a.$$

Intuitively, this means that f(x) can be made as close as desired to a by making x big enough. How big is big enough depends on how close one wishes to make f(x) to a.

a. Second derivative
b. Third derivative
c. Mountain pass theorem
d. Horizontal asymptote

30. The line x = a is a _____ of a curve y=f(x) if at least one of the following statements is true:

1. $\lim_{x \to a} f(x) = \pm\infty$
2. $\lim_{x \to a^-} f(x) = \pm\infty$
3. $\lim_{x \to a^+} f(x) = \pm\infty$

Intuitively, if x = a is an asymptote of f, then, if we imagine x approaching a from one side, the value of f(x) grows without bound; i.e., f(x) becomes large (positively or negatively), and, in fact, becomes larger than any finite value.

Note that f(x) may or may not be defined at a: what the function is doing precisely at x = a does not affect the asymptote. For example, consider the function

$$f(x) = \begin{cases} \frac{1}{x} & \text{if } x > 0, \\ 5 & \text{if } x \leq 0 \end{cases}$$

As $x \to 0^+$, $\lim f(x) = \infty$, f(x) has a _____ at 0, even though f(0) = 5.

Another example is $f(x) = 1/(x-1)$ which has a _____ of x=1 as shown by the limit

$$\lim_{x \to 1^+} \frac{1}{x-1} = \infty$$

In the graph of $f(x) = x + \frac{1}{x}$, the y-axis (x = 0) and the line y = x are both asymptotes.

When a linear asymptote is not parallel to the x- or y-axis, it is called either an oblique asymptote or equivalently a slant asymptote.

a. Ramp function
b. Monodromy
c. Third derivative
d. Vertical asymptote

Chapter 6. APPLICATIONS OF THE DERIVATIVE

1. The largest and the smallest element of a set are called extreme values, absolute extrema, or extreme records.

For a differentiable function f, if f(x_0) is an _____ for the set of all values f(x), and if x_0 is in the interior of the domain of f, then x_0 is a critical point, by Fermat's theorem.

In the case of a general partial order one should not confuse a least element (smaller than all other) and a minimal element (nothing is smaller.)

   a. Infinitesimal
   b. Integration by substitution
   c. Extreme Value Theorem
   d. Extreme value

2. In calculus, the _____ states that if a real-valued function f is continuous in the closed and bounded interval [a,b], then f must attain its maximum and minimum value, each at least once. That is, there exist numbers c and d in [a,b] such that:

$$f(c) \geq f(x) \geq f(d) \quad \text{for all } x \in [a, b].$$

A related theorem is the boundedness theorem which states that a continuous function f in the closed interval [a,b] is bounded on that interval. That is, there exist real numbers m and M such that:

$$m \leq f(x) \leq M \quad \text{for all } x \in [a, b].$$

The _____ enriches the boundedness theorem by saying that not only is the function bounded, but it also attains its least upper bound as its maximum and its greatest lower bound as its minimum.

   a. Infinitesimal
   b. Integral of secant cubed
   c. Uniform convergence
   d. Extreme value theorem

3. In a totally ordered set all elements are mutually comparable, so such a set can have at most one minimal element and at most one maximal element. Then, due to mutual comparability, the minimal element will also be the least element and the maximal element will also be the greatest element. Thus in a totally ordered set we can simply use the terms minimum and _____.

a. Nth term
b. Racetrack principle
c. Leibniz rule
d. Maximum

4. In a totally ordered set all elements are mutually comparable, so such a set can have at most one minimal element and at most one maximal element. Then, due to mutual comparability, the minimal element will also be the least element and the maximal element will also be the greatest element. Thus in a totally ordered set we can simply use the terms _____ and maximum.

a. Ghosts of departed quantities
b. Maximum
c. Nth term
d. Minimum

5. In mathematics, the simplest case of _____ refers to the study of problems in which one seeks to minimize or maximize a real function by systematically choosing the values of real or integer variables from within an allowed set. This (a scalar real valued objective function) is actually a small subset of this field which comprises a large area of applied mathematics and generalizes to study of means to obtain 'best available' values of some objective function given a defined domain where the elaboration is on the types of functions and the conditions and nature of the objects in the problem domain.

The first _____ technique, which is known as steepest descent, goes back to Gauss.

a. ACTRAN
b. ALGOR
c. AUSM
d. Optimization

6. In calculus, a branch of mathematics, the _____ is a measurement of how a function changes when its input changes. Loosely speaking, a _____ can be thought of as how much a quantity is changing at some given point. For example, the _____ of the position (or distance) of a vehicle with respect to time is the instantaneous velocity (respectively, instantaneous speed) at which the vehicle is traveling.

The process of finding a _____ is called differentiation. The fundamental theorem of calculus states that differentiation is the reverse process to integration.

Chapter 6. APPLICATIONS OF THE DERIVATIVE

a. Semi-differentiability
b. Stationary phase approximation
c. Bounded function
d. Derivative

7. The _____ of any solid, liquid, plasma, vacuum or theoretical object is how much three-dimensional space it occupies, often quantified numerically. One-dimensional figures (such as lines) and two-dimensional shapes (such as squares) are assigned zero _____ in the three-dimensional space. _____ is commonly presented in units such as mL or cm³ (milliliters or cubic centimeters.)
   a. Dirac equation
   b. Vector potential
   c. Klein-Gordon equation
   d. Volume

8. Just as the definite integral of a positive function of one variable represents the area of the region between the graph of the function and the x-axis, the _____ of a positive function of two variables represents the volume of the region between the surface defined by the function (on the three dimensional Cartesian plane where z = f(x,y)) and the plane which contains its domain. (Note that the same volume can be obtained via the triple integral -- the integral of a function in three variables -- of the constant function f(x, y, z) = 1 over the above-mentioned region between the surface and the plane.) If there are more variables, a multiple integral will yield hypervolumes of multi-dimensional functions.
   a. Trigonometric substitution
   b. Double integral
   c. Risch algorithm
   d. Constant of integration

9. Integration is an important concept in mathematics, specifically in the field of calculus and, more broadly, mathematical analysis. Given a function f of a real variable x and an interval [a, b] of the real line, the _____

$$\int_a^b f(x)\, dx,$$

is defined informally to be the net signed area of the region in the xy-plane bounded by the graph of f, the x-axis, and the vertical lines x = a and x = b.

The term '_____' may also refer to the notion of antiderivative, a function F whose derivative is the given function f.

a. Integrand
b. Integral test for convergence
c. Indefinite integral
d. Integral

10. In calculus, a method called _____ can be applied to implicitly defined functions. This method is an application of the chain rule allowing one to calculate the derivative of a function given implicitly.

As explained in the introduction, y can be given as a function of x implicitly rather than explicitly. When we have an equation R (x,y) = 0, we may be able to solve it for y and then differentiate. However, sometimes it is simpler to differentiate R(x,y) with respect to x and then solve for dy / dx.

a. Implicit differentiation
b. Implicit function
c. Ordinary differential equation
d. Automatic differentiation

11. In Geometry, the _____ is an algebraic curve defined by the equation

$$x^3 + y^3 - 3axy = 0$$

It forms a loop in the first quadrant with a double point at the origin and asymptote

$$x + y + a = 0$$

It is symmetrical about y = x.

a. Cochleoid
b. Folium of Descartes
c. Prolate cycloid
d. Curve

12. _____ is used to describe the steepness, incline, gradient, or grade of a straight line. A higher _____ value indicates a steeper incline. The _____ is defined as the ratio of the 'rise' divided by the 'run' between two points on a line, or in other words, the ratio of the altitude change to the horizontal distance between any two points on the line.

Chapter 6. APPLICATIONS OF THE DERIVATIVE

a. 15 theorem
b. Y-intercept
c. Sequence
d. Slope

13. In geometry, the _____ (or simply the tangent) to a curve at a given point is the straight line that 'just touches' the curve at that point (in the sense explained more precisely below.) As it passes through the point of tangency, the _____ is 'going in the same direction' as the curve, and in this sense it is the best straight-line approximation to the curve at that point. The same definition applies to space curves and curves in n-dimensional Euclidean space.
   a. Lie derivative
   b. North pole
   c. Minimal surface
   d. Tangent line

14. Trigonometry is a branch of mathematics that deals with triangles, particularly those plane triangles in which one angle has 90 degrees (right triangles.) Trigonometry deals with relationships between the sides and the angles of triangles and with the _____ functions, which describe those relationships.

Trigonometry has applications in both pure mathematics and in applied mathematics, where it is essential in many branches of science and technology.

   a. Trigonometric functions
   b. Sine
   c. Trigonometric
   d. Trigonometric integrals

15. In mathematics, the _____ are functions of an angle. They are important in the study of triangles and modeling periodic phenomena, among many other applications. _____ are commonly defined as ratios of two sides of a right triangle containing the angle, and can equivalently be defined as the lengths of various line segments from a unit circle.
   a. Trigonometric
   b. Sine integral
   c. Trigonometric integrals
   d. Trigonometric functions

16. The method of _____ or ordinary _____ is used to solve overdetermined systems. _____ is often applied in statistical contexts, particularly regression analysis.

_____ can be interpreted as a method of fitting data. The best fit in the _____ sense is that instance of the model for which the sum of squared residuals has its least value, a residual being the difference between an observed value and the value given by the model.

a. BIBO stability
b. BDDC
c. 15 theorem
d. Least squares

17.

In differential calculus, _____ problems involve finding a rate that a quantity changes by relating the population of the earth. The rate of change is usually with respect to people who have died.

a. Visual Calculus
b. Standard part function
c. Mean Value Theorem
d. Related rates

18.   In mathematics, a _____ is an approximation of a general function using a linear function (more precisely, an affine function.)

Given a differentiable function f of one real variable, Taylor's theorem for n=1 states that

$$f(x) = f(a) + f\,'(a)(x-a) + R_2$$

where R_2 is the remainder term. The _____ is obtained by dropping the remainder:

$$f(x) \approx f(a) + f\,'(a)(x-a)$$

which is true for x close to a.

a. Point of inflection
b. Lin-Tsien equation
c. Smooth function
d. Linear approximation

19. In infinitesimal calculus, a _____ is traditionally an infinitesimally small change in a variable. For example, if x is a variable, then a change in the value of x is often denoted Δx (or δx when this change is considered to be small.) The _____ dx represents such a change, but is infinitely small.

  a. Dirichlet integral
  b. Differential
  c. Local maximum
  d. The Method of Mechanical Theorems

Chapter 7. INTEGRATION

1. In calculus, an _____, primitive or indefinite integral of a function f is a function F whose derivative is equal to f, i.e., F >' = f. The process of solving for antiderivatives is antidifferentiation (or indefinite integration.) Antiderivatives are related to definite integrals through the fundamental theorem of calculus: the definite integral of a function over an interval is equal to the difference between the values of an _____ evaluated at the endpoints of the interval.
   a. Order of integration
   b. Indefinite integral
   c. Integrand
   d. Antiderivative

2. In mathematics, a (topological) _____ is defined as follows: let I be an interval of real numbers (i.e. a non-empty connected subset of $\mathbb{R}$); then a _____ γ is a continuous mapping $\gamma : I \to X$, where X is a topological space. The _____ γ is said to be simple if it is injective, i.e. if for all x, y in I, we have $\gamma(x) = \gamma(y) \implies x = y$. If I is a closed bounded interval $[a, b]$, we also allow the possibility $\gamma(a) = \gamma(b)$ (this convention makes it possible to talk about closed simple _____.)
   a. Prolate cycloid
   b. Tractrix
   c. Closed curve
   d. Curve

3. Integration is an important concept in mathematics, specifically in the field of calculus and, more broadly, mathematical analysis. Given a function f of a real variable x and an interval [a, b] of the real line, the _____

$$\int_a^b f(x)\,dx,$$

is defined informally to be the net signed area of the region in the xy-plane bounded by the graph of f, the x-axis, and the vertical lines x = a and x = b.

The term '_____' may also refer to the notion of antiderivative, a function F whose derivative is the given function f.

   a. Indefinite integral
   b. Integrand
   c. Integral test for convergence
   d. Integral

4. In calculus, a branch of mathematics, the _____ is a measurement of how a function changes when its input changes. Loosely speaking, a _____ can be thought of as how much a quantity is changing at some given point. For example, the _____ of the position (or distance) of a vehicle with respect to time is the instantaneous velocity (respectively, instantaneous speed) at which the vehicle is traveling.

Chapter 7. INTEGRATION

The process of finding a _____ is called differentiation. The fundamental theorem of calculus states that differentiation is the reverse process to integration.

a. Stationary phase approximation
b. Bounded function
c. Semi-differentiability
d. Derivative

5. In infinitesimal calculus, a _____ is traditionally an infinitesimally small change in a variable. For example, if x is a variable, then a change in the value of x is often denoted Δx (or δx when this change is considered to be small.) The _____ dx represents such a change, but is infinitely small.

a. Local maximum
b. Differential
c. The Method of Mechanical Theorems
d. Dirichlet integral

6. _____, a field in mathematics, is the study of how functions change when their inputs change. The primary object of study in _____ is the derivative. A closely related notion is the differential.

a. Concave downwards
b. Ramp function
c. Differential calculus
d. Slant asymptote

7. The _____ specifies the relationship between the two central operations of calculus, differentiation and integration.

The first part of the theorem, sometimes called the first _____, shows that an indefinite integration can be reversed by a differentiation.

The second part, sometimes called the second _____, allows one to compute the definite integral of a function by using any one of its infinitely many antiderivatives.

a. Fundamental Theorem of Calculus
b. Leibniz formula
c. Periodic function
d. Limits of integration

Chapter 7. INTEGRATION

8. _____ is any physical or virtual entity that is owned by an individual or jointly by a group of individuals. An owner of _____ has the right to consume, sell, rent, mortgage, transfer and exchange his or her _____. Important widely-recognized types of _____ include real _____, personal _____ (other physical possessions), and intellectual _____ (rights over artistic creations, inventions, etc.), although the latter is not always as widely recognized or enforced.
   a. BDDC
   b. 15 theorem
   c. BIBO stability
   d. Property

9. In calculus, an antiderivative, primitive or _____ of a function f is a function F whose derivative is equal to f, i.e., F ' = f. The process of solving for antiderivatives is antidifferentiation (or indefinite integration.) Antiderivatives are related to definite integrals through the fundamental theorem of calculus: the definite integral of a function over an interval is equal to the difference between the values of an antiderivative evaluated at the endpoints of the interval.
   a. Integral test for convergence
   b. Integration by parts operator
   c. Arc length
   d. Indefinite integral

10. If a function has an integral, it is said to be integrable. The function for which the integral is calculated is called the _____. The region over which a function is being integrated is called the domain of integration.
    a. Integrand
    b. Integration by parts
    c. Integral test for convergence
    d. Order of integration

11. This article will state and prove the _____ for differentiation, and then use it to prove these two formulas.

The _____ for differentiation states that for every natural number n, the derivative of $f(x) = x^n$ is $f'(x) = nx^{n-1}$, that is,

$$(x^n)' = nx^{n-1}.$$

The _____ for integration

$$\int x^n \, dx = \frac{x^{n+1}}{n+1} + C$$

for natural n is then an easy consequence. One just needs to take the derivative of this equality and use the _____ and linearity of differentiation on the right-hand side.

a. Functional integration
b. Power rule
c. Test for Divergence
d. Leibniz rule

12. _____ is a type of motion in which the velocity of an object changes equal amounts in equal time periods. An example of an object having _____ would be a ball rolling down a ramp. The object picks up velocity as it goes down the ramp with equal changes in time.

a. AUSM
b. ALGOR
c. ACTRAN
d. Uniform Acceleration

13. In calculus, the _____ allows you to take constants outside a derivative and concentrate on differentiating the function of x itself. This is a part of the linearity of differentiation.

Suppose you have a function

$$g(x) = k \cdot f(x).$$

where k is a constant.

Use the formula for differentiation from first principles to obtain:

$$g'(x) = \lim_{h \to 0} \frac{g(x+h) - g(x)}{h}$$
$$g'(x) = \lim_{h \to 0} \frac{k \cdot f(x+h) - k \cdot f(x)}{h}$$
$$g'(x) = \lim_{h \to 0} \frac{k(f(x+h) - f(x))}{h}$$
$$g'(x) = k \lim_{h \to 0} \frac{f(x+h) - f(x)}{h} \quad (*)$$
$$g'(x) = k \cdot f'(x).$$

This is the statement of the _____, in Lagrange's notation for differentiation.

a. Reciprocal Rule
b. Quotient Rule
c. Product rule
d. Constant factor rule in differentiation

14. The _____ is a function in mathematics. The application of this function to a value x is written as exp(x). Equivalently, this can be written in the form e^x, where e is a mathematical constant, the base of the natural logarithm, which equals approximately 2.718281828, and is also known as Euler's number.

a. Area hyperbolic functions
b. Integral part
c. ACTRAN
d. Exponential function

15. _____ is the concept of adding accumulated interest back to the principal, so that interest is earned on interest from that moment on. The act of declaring interest to be principal is called compounding (i.e., interest is compounded.) A loan, for example, may have its interest compounded every month: in this case, a loan with $100 principal and 1% interest per month would have a balance of $101 at the end of the first month.

a. BIBO stability
b. 15 theorem
c. BDDC
d. Compound interest

16. In mathematics, the _____ (or modulus) of a real number is its numerical value without regard to its sign. So, for example, 3 is the _____ of both 3 and −3.

The _____ of a number a is denoted by $|a|$.

a. ACTRAN
b. Area hyperbolic functions
c. Exponential function
d. Absolute value

17. In physics, _____ is defined as the rate of change of position. it is vector physical quantity; both speed and direction are required to define it. In the SI (metric) system, it is measured in meters per second: (m/s) or ms^{-1}.

a. Velocity
b. BDDC
c. 15 theorem
d. BIBO stability

18. In mathematics, a _____ is a polynomial equation of the second degree. The general form is

$$ax^2 + bx + c = 0,$$

where a ≠ 0.

Students and teachers all over the world are familiar with the quadratic formula that can be derived by completing the square.

a. Stern-Brocot tree
b. Continued fraction
c. Quadratic equation
d. Lochs' theorem

19. A quadratic equation with real or complex coefficients has two solutions (or roots), not necessarily distinct, which may or may not be real, given by the _____:

$$\frac{-b \pm \sqrt{b^2 - 4ac}}{2a}$$

Example discriminant signsâ— <0: $x^2 + \frac{1}{2}$â— =0: $-\frac{4}{3}x^2 + \frac{4}{3}x - \frac{1}{3}$ â— >0: $\frac{3}{2}x^2 + \frac{1}{2}x - \frac{4}{3}$

In the above formula, the expression underneath the square root sign

$$D = b^2 - 4ac,$$

is called the discriminant of the quadratic equation.

A quadratic equation with real coefficients can have either one or two distinct real roots, or two distinct complex roots. In this case the discriminant determines the number and nature of the roots.

a. Quadratic formula
b. Quartic function
c. Linear equation
d. Cubic function

20. In a totally ordered set all elements are mutually comparable, so such a set can have at most one minimal element and at most one maximal element. Then, due to mutual comparability, the minimal element will also be the least element and the maximal element will also be the greatest element. Thus in a totally ordered set we can simply use the terms minimum and _____.

a. Nth term
b. Leibniz rule
c. Racetrack principle
d. Maximum

21. In calculus, the _____ is a formula for the derivative of the composite of two functions.

In intuitive terms, if a variable, y, depends on a second variable, u, which in turn depends on a third variable, x, then the rate of change of y with respect to x can be computed as the rate of change of y with respect to u multiplied by the rate of change of u with respect to x. Schematically,

$$\frac{dy}{dx} = \frac{dy}{du} \cdot \frac{du}{dx}.$$

a. Reciprocal Rule
b. Differentiation rules
c. Product rule
d. Chain rule

22. A _____ officer is an officer of high military rank. The term or equivalent is used by nearly every country in the world. _____ can be used as a generic term for all grades of _____ officer, or it can specifically refer to a single rank that is just called _____.

a. 15 theorem
b. General
c. BIBO stability
d. BDDC

Chapter 7. INTEGRATION

23. In mathematics, the _____ is a conic section, the intersection of a right circular conical surface and a plane parallel to a generating straight line of that surface. Given a point (the focus) and a line (the directrix) that lie in a plane, the locus of points in that plane that are equidistant to them is a _____.

A particular case arises when the plane is tangent to the conical surface of a circle.

a. 15 theorem
b. BDDC
c. Parabola
d. BIBO stability

24. In mathematics, the _____ is a way to approximately calculate the definite integral

$$\int_a^b f(x)\,dx.$$

The _____ works by approximating the region under the graph of the function f by a trapezoid and calculating its area. It follows that

$$\int_a^b f(x)\,dx \approx (b-a)\frac{f(a)+f(b)}{2}.$$

To calculate this integral more accurately, one first splits the interval of integration [a,b] into n smaller subintervals, and then applies the _____ on each of them. One obtains the composite _____:

$$\int_a^b f(x)\,dx \approx \frac{b-a}{n}\left[\frac{f(a)+f(b)}{2} + \sum_{k=1}^{n-1} f\left(a + k\frac{b-a}{n}\right)\right].$$

This can alternatively be written as:

$$\int_a^b f(x)\,dx \approx \frac{b-a}{2n}\left(f(x_0) + 2f(x_1) + 2f(x_2) + \cdots + 2f(x_{n-1}) + f(x_n)\right)$$

where

$$x_k = a + k\frac{b-a}{n}, \quad \text{for } k = 0, 1, \ldots, n$$

(one can also use a non-uniform grid.)

Chapter 7. INTEGRATION

a. BIBO stability
b. BDDC
c. 15 theorem
d. Trapezoidal rule

25. In elementary algebra, a _____ is a polynomial with two terms--the sum of two monomials--often bound by parenthesis or brackets when operated upon. It is the simplest kind of polynomial other than monomials.

- The _____ $a^2 - b^2$ can be factored as the product of two other binomials:

    $a^2 - b^2 = (a + b)(a - b.)$

    This is a special case of the more general formula:

    $$a^{n+1} - b^{n+1} = (a - b) \sum_{k=0}^{n} a^k b^{n-k}$$

- The product of a pair of linear binomials $(ax + b)$ and $(cx + d)$ is:

    $(ax + b)(cx + d) = acx^2 + axd + bcx + bd.$

- A _____ raised to the nth power, represented as

    $(a + b)^n$

    can be expanded by means of the _____ theorem or, equivalently, using Pascal's triangle. Taking a simple example, the perfect square _____ $(p + q)^2$ can be found by squaring the :first digit, adding twice the product of the first and second digit and finally adding the square of the second digit, to give $p^2 + 2pq + q^2$.

a. Completing the square
b. Multinomial theorem
c. Binomial
d. Partial fractions

26. In mathematics, the concept of a '_____' is used to describe the behavior of a function as its argument or input either 'gets close' to some point, or as the argument becomes arbitrarily large; or the behavior of a sequence's elements as their index increases indefinitely. Limits are used in calculus and other branches of mathematical analysis to define derivatives and continuity.

In formulas, _____ is usually abbreviated as lim

a. BIBO stability
b. 15 theorem
c. BDDC
d. Limit

27. In mathematics, a _____ is a method for approximating the total area underneath a curve on a graph, otherwise known as an integral. It may also be used to define the integration operation.

Consider a function $f: D \longrightarrow R$, where D is a subset of the real numbers R, and let $I = [a, b]$ be a closed interval contained in D. A finite set of points $\{x_0, x_1, x_2, ... x_n\}$ such that $a = x_0 < x_1 < x_2 ... < x_n = b$ creates a partition

$$P = \{[x_0, x_1], [x_1, x_2], ... [x_{n-1}, x_n]\}$$

of I.

a. Signed measure
b. Risch algorithm
c. Solid of revolution
d. Riemann sum

28. In calculus and mathematical analysis the _____ of the integral

$$\int_a^b f(x)\,dx$$

of a Riemann integrable function f defined on a closed and bounded interval [a, b] are the real numbers a and b.

_____ can also be defined for improper integrals, with the _____ of both

$$\lim_{z \to a^+} \int_z^b f(x)\,dx$$

and

$$\lim_{z \to b^-} \int_a^z f(x)\,dx$$

again being a and b. For an improper integral

$$\int_a^\infty f(x)\,dx$$

or

$$\int_{-\infty}^b f(x)\,dx$$

the _____ are a and ∞, or −∞ and b, respectively.

- a. Test for Divergence
- b. Maxima
- c. Differential
- d. Limits of Integration

29. In mathematics, the simplest case of _____ refers to the study of problems in which one seeks to minimize or maximize a real function by systematically choosing the values of real or integer variables from within an allowed set. This (a scalar real valued objective function) is actually a small subset of this field which comprises a large area of applied mathematics and generalizes to study of means to obtain 'best available' values of some objective function given a defined domain where the elaboration is on the types of functions and the conditions and nature of the objects in the problem domain.

The first _____ technique, which is known as steepest descent, goes back to Gauss.

- a. ALGOR
- b. ACTRAN
- c. AUSM
- d. Optimization

30. In numerical analysis, _____ constitutes a broad family of algorithms for calculating the numerical value of a definite integral, and by extension, the term is also sometimes used to describe the numerical solution of differential equations The term numerical quadrature is more or less a synonym for _____, especially as applied to one-dimensional integrals.

a. Meshfree methods
b. Galerkin methods
c. Numerical integration
d. Multigrid method

31. In calculus, _____ gives a sequence of approximations of a differentiable function around a given point by polynomials (the Taylor polynomials of that function) whose coefficients depend only on the derivatives of the function at that point. The theorem also gives precise estimates on the size of the error in the approximation. The theorem is named after the mathematician Brook Taylor, who stated it in 1712, though the result was first discovered 41 years earlier in 1671 by James Gregory.

a. Local minimum
b. Fresnel integrals
c. Related rates
d. Taylor's theorem

32. _____ is the study of algorithms for the problems of continuous mathematics (as distinguished from discrete mathematics.)

One of the earliest mathematical writings is the Babylonian tablet YBC 7289, which gives a sexagesimal numerical approximation of $\sqrt{2}$, the length of the diagonal in a unit square. Being able to compute the sides of a triangle (and hence, being able to compute square roots) is extremely important, for instance, in carpentry and construction.

a. BIBO stability
b. BDDC
c. 15 theorem
d. Numerical analysis

Chapter 8. FURTHER TECHNIQUES AND APPLICATIONS OF INTEGRATION

1. In calculus, an _____ is the limit of a definite integral as an endpoint of the interval of integration approaches either a specified real number or ∞ or −∞ or, in some cases, as both endpoints approach limits.

Specifically, an _____ is a limit of the form

$$\lim_{b \to \infty} \int_a^b f(x)\,dx, \qquad \lim_{a \to -\infty} \int_a^b f(x)\,dx,$$

or of the form

$$\lim_{c \to b^-} \int_a^c f(x)\,dx, \qquad \lim_{c \to a^+} \int_c^b f(x)\,dx,$$

in which one takes a limit in one or the other (or sometimes both) endpoints. Improper integrals may also occur at an interior point of the domain of integration, or at multiple such points.

a. ACTRAN
b. AUSM
c. ALGOR
d. Improper integral

2. Integration is an important concept in mathematics, specifically in the field of calculus and, more broadly, mathematical analysis. Given a function f of a real variable x and an interval [a, b] of the real line, the _____

$$\int_a^b f(x)\,dx,$$

is defined informally to be the net signed area of the region in the xy-plane bounded by the graph of f, the x-axis, and the vertical lines x = a and x = b.

The term '_____' may also refer to the notion of antiderivative, a function F whose derivative is the given function f.

a. Integral test for convergence
b. Integrand
c. Indefinite integral
d. Integral

Chapter 8. FURTHER TECHNIQUES AND APPLICATIONS OF INTEGRATION

3. In mathematics, a (topological) _____ is defined as follows: let I be an interval of real numbers (i.e. a non-empty connected subset of $\mathbb{R}$); then a _____ γ is a continuous mapping $\gamma : I \to X$, where X is a topological space. The _____ γ is said to be simple if it is injective, i.e. if for all x, y in I, we have $\gamma(x) = \gamma(y) \implies x = y$. If I is a closed bounded interval $[a, b]$, we also allow the possibility $\gamma(a) = \gamma(b)$ (this convention makes it possible to talk about closed simple _____.)
    a. Closed curve
    b. Prolate cycloid
    c. Tractrix
    d. Curve

4. In a totally ordered set all elements are mutually comparable, so such a set can have at most one minimal element and at most one maximal element. Then, due to mutual comparability, the minimal element will also be the least element and the maximal element will also be the greatest element. Thus in a totally ordered set we can simply use the terms minimum and _____.
    a. Nth term
    b. Leibniz rule
    c. Racetrack principle
    d. Maximum

5. In calculus, the _____ is a formula for the derivative of the composite of two functions.

In intuitive terms, if a variable, y, depends on a second variable, u, which in turn depends on a third variable, x, then the rate of change of y with respect to x can be computed as the rate of change of y with respect to u multiplied by the rate of change of u with respect to x. Schematically,

$$\frac{dy}{dx} = \frac{dy}{du} \cdot \frac{du}{dx}.$$

   a. Product rule
   b. Chain rule
   c. Reciprocal Rule
   d. Differentiation rules

6. In calculus, and more generally in mathematical analysis, _____ is a rule that transforms the integral of products of functions into other, hopefully simpler, integrals. The rule arises from the product rule of differentiation.

Chapter 8. FURTHER TECHNIQUES AND APPLICATIONS OF INTEGRATION

If u = f(x), v = g(x), and the differentials du = f '(x) dx and dv = g'(x) dx; then in its simplest form the product rule is:

$$\int u\,dv = uv - \int v\,du.$$

Suppose f(x) and g(x) are two continuously differentiable functions.

a. Arc length
b. Integration by parametric derivatives
c. Integration by parts
d. Integrand

7. In computer science and information science, _____ could also be a method or an algorithm. Again, an example will illustrate: There are systems of counting, as with Roman numerals, and various systems for filing papers, or catalogues, and various library systems, of which the Dewey Decimal _____ is an example. This still fits with the definition of components which are connected together (in this case in order to facilitate the flow of information.)

a. BIBO stability
b. 15 theorem
c. System
d. BDDC

8. In mathematics, engineering, and manufacturing, a _____ is a solid figure obtained by rotating a plane curve around some straight line (the axis) that lies on the same plane.

Assuming that the curve does not cross the axis, the solid's volume is equal to the length of the circle described by the figure's centroid, times the figure's area (Pappus's second centroid Theorem.)

Rotating a curve

A representative disk is a three-dimensional volume element of a _____.

a. Trigonometric substitution
b. Solid of revolution
c. Riemann sum
d. Surface of revolution

Chapter 8. FURTHER TECHNIQUES AND APPLICATIONS OF INTEGRATION

9. The _____ of any solid, liquid, plasma, vacuum or theoretical object is how much three-dimensional space it occupies, often quantified numerically. One-dimensional figures (such as lines) and two-dimensional shapes (such as squares) are assigned zero _____ in the three-dimensional space. _____ is commonly presented in units such as mL or cm^3 (milliliters or cubic centimeters.)
   a. Klein-Gordon equation
   b. Dirac equation
   c. Volume
   d. Vector potential

10. Just as the definite integral of a positive function of one variable represents the area of the region between the graph of the function and the x-axis, the _____ of a positive function of two variables represents the volume of the region between the surface defined by the function (on the three dimensional Cartesian plane where z = f(x,y)) and the plane which contains its domain. (Note that the same volume can be obtained via the triple integral -- the integral of a function in three variables -- of the constant function f(x, y, z) = 1 over the above-mentioned region between the surface and the plane.) If there are more variables, a multiple integral will yield hypervolumes of multi-dimensional functions.
   a. Risch algorithm
   b. Trigonometric substitution
   c. Constant of integration
   d. Double integral

11. _____ was a German mathematician, astronomer and astrologer, and key figure in the 17th century scientific revolution. He is best known for his eponymous laws of planetary motion, codified by later astronomers based on his works Astronomia nova, Harmonices Mundi, and Epitome of Copernican Astrononomy. They also provided one of the foundations for Isaac Newton's theory of universal gravitation.
   a. MÄ dhava of Sangamagrama
   b. Johannes Kepler
   c. Niels Henrik David Bohr
   d. Robin K. Bullough

12. In calculus, an _____, primitive or indefinite integral of a function f is a function F whose derivative is equal to f, i.e., F >' = f. The process of solving for antiderivatives is antidifferentiation (or indefinite integration.) Antiderivatives are related to definite integrals through the fundamental theorem of calculus: the definite integral of a function over an interval is equal to the difference between the values of an _____ evaluated at the endpoints of the interval.
   a. Order of integration
   b. Indefinite integral
   c. Antiderivative
   d. Integrand

Chapter 8. FURTHER TECHNIQUES AND APPLICATIONS OF INTEGRATION

13. The _____ specifies the relationship between the two central operations of calculus, differentiation and integration.

The first part of the theorem, sometimes called the first _____, shows that an indefinite integration can be reversed by a differentiation.

The second part, sometimes called the second _____, allows one to compute the definite integral of a function by using any one of its infinitely many antiderivatives.

   a. Periodic function
   b. Limits of integration
   c. Leibniz formula
   d. Fundamental Theorem of Calculus

14. In mathematics, the concept of a '_____' is used to describe the behavior of a function as its argument or input either 'gets close' to some point, or as the argument becomes arbitrarily large; or the behavior of a sequence's elements as their index increases indefinitely. Limits are used in calculus and other branches of mathematical analysis to define derivatives and continuity.

In formulas, _____ is usually abbreviated as lim

   a. 15 theorem
   b. BDDC
   c. BIBO stability
   d. Limit

15. _____ is any physical or virtual entity that is owned by an individual or jointly by a group of individuals. An owner of _____ has the right to consume, sell, rent, mortgage, transfer and exchange his or her _____. Important widely-recognized types of _____ include real _____, personal _____ (other physical possessions), and intellectual _____ (rights over artistic creations, inventions, etc.), although the latter is not always as widely recognized or enforced.
   a. Property
   b. 15 theorem
   c. BIBO stability
   d. BDDC

16. In infinitesimal calculus, a _____ is traditionally an infinitesimally small change in a variable. For example, if x is a variable, then a change in the value of x is often denoted Δx (or δx when this change is considered to be small.) The _____ dx represents such a change, but is infinitely small.

Chapter 8. FURTHER TECHNIQUES AND APPLICATIONS OF INTEGRATION

a. Local maximum
b. Dirichlet integral
c. Differential
d. The Method of Mechanical Theorems

17. A _____ is a mathematical equation for an unknown function of one or several variables that relates the values of the function itself and of its derivatives of various orders. they play a prominent role in engineering, physics, economics and other disciplines.

A simplified real world example of a _____ is modeling the acceleration of a ball falling through the air (considering only gravity and air resistance.)

a. Differential equation
b. Structural stability
c. Phase line
d. Caloric polynomial

Chapter 9. MULTIVARIABLE CALCULUS

1. In mathematics, a _____ of a function of several variables is its derivative with respect to one of those variables with the others held constant (as opposed to the total derivative, in which all variables are allowed to vary.) Partial derivatives are useful in vector calculus and differential geometry.

The _____ of a function f with respect to the variable x is written as f'_x, $\partial_x f$, or $\partial f/\partial x$.

   a. Jacobian
   b. Differentiation operator
   c. Level curve
   d. Partial derivative

2. In calculus, a branch of mathematics, the _____ is a measurement of how a function changes when its input changes. Loosely speaking, a _____ can be thought of as how much a quantity is changing at some given point. For example, the _____ of the position (or distance) of a vehicle with respect to time is the instantaneous velocity (respectively, instantaneous speed) at which the vehicle is traveling.

The process of finding a _____ is called differentiation. The fundamental theorem of calculus states that differentiation is the reverse process to integration.

   a. Stationary phase approximation
   b. Semi-differentiability
   c. Derivative
   d. Bounded function

3. The terms '_____' and 'independent variable' are used in similar but subtly different ways in mathematics and statistics as part of the standard terminology in those subjects. They are used to distinguish between two types of quantities being considered, separating them into those available at the start of a process and those being created by it, where the latter (dependent variables) are dependent on the former (independent variables.)

In traditional calculus, a function is defined as a relation between two terms called variables because their values vary.

   a. BIBO stability
   b. BDDC
   c. 15 theorem
   d. Dependent variable

Chapter 9. MULTIVARIABLE CALCULUS

4. In mathematics, the _____ (or replacement set) of a given function is the set of 'input' values for which the function is defined. For instance, the _____ of cosine would be all real numbers, while the _____ of the square root would be only numbers greater than or equal to 0 (ignoring complex numbers in both cases.) In a representation of a function in a xy Cartesian coordinate system, the _____ is represented on the x axis (or abscissa.)
    a. BIBO stability
    b. 15 theorem
    c. BDDC
    d. Domain

5. The terms 'dependent variable' and '_____' are used in similar but subtly different ways in mathematics and statistics as part of the standard terminology in those subjects. They are used to distinguish between two types of quantities being considered, separating them into those available at the start of a process and those being created by it, where the latter (dependent variables) are dependent on the former (independent variables.)

In traditional calculus, a function is defined as a relation between two terms called variables because their values vary.

   a. AUSM
   b. ALGOR
   c. ACTRAN
   d. Independent variable

6. In mathematics, the _____ of a function is the set of all 'output' values produced by that function. Sometimes it is called the image, or more precisely, the image of the domain of the function. If a function is a surjection then its _____ is equal to its codomain.
    a. Surjective
    b. Constant function
    c. Range
    d. Piecewise-defined function

7. In mathematics, a (topological) _____ is defined as follows: let I be an interval of real numbers (i.e. a non-empty connected subset of $\mathbb{R}$); then a _____ γ is a continuous mapping $\gamma : I \to X$, where X is a topological space. The _____ γ is said to be simple if it is injective, i.e. if for all x, y in I, we have $\gamma(x) = \gamma(y) \implies x = y$. If I is a closed bounded interval $[a, b]$, we also allow the possibility $\gamma(a) = \gamma(b)$ (this convention makes it possible to talk about closed simple _____ .)

a. Prolate cycloid
b. Tractrix
c. Curve
d. Closed curve

8. When the number of variables is two, this is a _____, if it is three this is a level surface, and for higher values of n the level set is a level hypersurface.

More specifically, a _____ is the set of all real-valued roots of an equation in two variables x_1 and x_2. A level surface is the set of all real-valued roots of an equation in three variables x_1, x_2 and x_3.

a. Multipole moment
b. Scalar field
c. Level curve
d. Partial derivative

9. In mathematics, a _____ is a quadric surface of special kind. There are two kinds of paraboloids: elliptic and hyperbolic. The elliptic _____ is shaped like an oval cup and can have a maximum or minimum point.
a. Hyperbolic paraboloid
b. Paraboloid
c. Torus
d. PDE surfaces

10. In economics, the _____ functional form of production functions is widely used to represent the relationship of an output to inputs. It was proposed by Knut Wicksell (1851-1926), and tested against statistical evidence by Charles Cobb and Paul Douglas in 1900-1928.

For production, the function is

$$Y = AL^{\alpha}K^{\beta},$$

where:

- Y = total production (the monetary value of all goods produced in a year)
- L = labor input
- K = capital input
- A = total factor productivity
- α and β are the output elasticities of labor and capital, respectively. These values are constants determined by available technology.

Output elasticity measures the responsiveness of output to a change in levels of either labor or capital used in production, ceteris paribus. For example if α = 0.15, a 1% increase in labor would lead to approximately a 0.15% increase in output.

a. BDDC
b. 15 theorem
c. BIBO stability
d. Cobb-Douglas

11. An _____ is a type of quadric surface that is a higher dimensional analogue of an ellipse. The equation of a standard axis-aligned _____ body in an xyz-Cartesian coordinate system is

$$\frac{x^2}{a^2} + \frac{y^2}{b^2} + \frac{z^2}{c^2} = 1$$

where a and b are the equatorial radii (along the x and y axes) and c is the polar radius (along the z-axis), all of which are fixed positive real numbers determining the shape of the _____.

More generally, a not-necessarily-axis-aligned _____ is defined by the equation

$$\mathbf{x}^T A \mathbf{x} = 1$$

where A is a symmetric positive definite matrix and x is a vector.

a. ACTRAN
b. AUSM
c. ALGOR
d. Ellipsoid

Chapter 9. MULTIVARIABLE CALCULUS

12. The _____ is a doubly ruled surface shaped like a saddle. In a suitable coordinate system, it can be represented by the equation

$$z = \frac{x^2}{a^2} - \frac{y^2}{b^2}.$$

This is a _____ that opens up along the x-axis and down along the y-axis.

Paraboloid of revolution

With a = b an elliptic paraboloid is a paraboloid of revolution: a surface obtained by revolving a parabola around its axis.

   a. Torus
   b. Paraboloid
   c. Parametric surface
   d. Hyperbolic paraboloid

13. In a totally ordered set all elements are mutually comparable, so such a set can have at most one minimal element and at most one maximal element. Then, due to mutual comparability, the minimal element will also be the least element and the maximal element will also be the greatest element. Thus in a totally ordered set we can simply use the terms minimum and _____.

   a. Nth term
   b. Racetrack principle
   c. Leibniz rule
   d. Maximum

14. In calculus, the _____ is a formula for the derivative of the composite of two functions.

In intuitive terms, if a variable, y, depends on a second variable, u, which in turn depends on a third variable, x, then the rate of change of y with respect to x can be computed as the rate of change of y with respect to u multiplied by the rate of change of u with respect to x. Schematically,

$$\frac{dy}{dx} = \frac{dy}{du} \cdot \frac{du}{dx}.$$

Chapter 9. MULTIVARIABLE CALCULUS

   a. Chain rule
   b. Reciprocal Rule
   c. Product rule
   d. Differentiation rules

15. The _____, formerly known as the hyperbolic logarithm, is the logarithm to the base e, where e is an irrational constant approximately equal to 2.718281828. It is also sometimes referred to as the Napierian logarithm, although the original meaning of this term is slightly different. In simple terms, the _____ of a number x is the power to which e would have to be raised to equal x -- for example the natural log of e itself is 1 because e^1 = e, while the _____ of 1 would be 0, since e^0 = 1.
   a. BDDC
   b. 15 theorem
   c. BIBO stability
   d. Natural logarithm

16. The function $\log_b(x)$ depends on both b and x, but the term _____ in standard usage refers to a function of the form $\log_b(x)$ in which the base b is fixed and so the only argument is x. Thus there is one _____ for each value of the base b (which must be positive and must differ from 1.) Viewed in this way, the base-b _____ is the inverse function of the exponential function b^x.
   a. BIBO stability
   b. BDDC
   c. 15 theorem
   d. Logarithm function

17. In geometry, the _____ (or simply the tangent) to a curve at a given point is the straight line that 'just touches' the curve at that point (in the sense explained more precisely below.) As it passes through the point of tangency, the _____ is 'going in the same direction' as the curve, and in this sense it is the best straight-line approximation to the curve at that point. The same definition applies to space curves and curves in n-dimensional Euclidean space.
   a. Minimal surface
   b. Lie derivative
   c. North pole
   d. Tangent line

18. Trigonometry is a branch of mathematics that deals with triangles, particularly those plane triangles in which one angle has 90 degrees (right triangles.) Trigonometry deals with relationships between the sides and the angles of triangles and with the _____ functions, which describe those relationships.

Trigonometry has applications in both pure mathematics and in applied mathematics, where it is essential in many branches of science and technology.

a. Sine
b. Trigonometric integrals
c. Trigonometric functions
d. Trigonometric

19. In mathematics, the _____ are functions of an angle. They are important in the study of triangles and modeling periodic phenomena, among many other applications. _____ are commonly defined as ratios of two sides of a right triangle containing the angle, and can equivalently be defined as the lengths of various line segments from a unit circle.

a. Sine integral
b. Trigonometric integrals
c. Trigonometric
d. Trigonometric functions

20. In a totally ordered set all elements are mutually comparable, so such a set can have at most one minimal element and at most one maximal element. Then, due to mutual comparability, the minimal element will also be the least element and the maximal element will also be the greatest element. Thus in a totally ordered set we can simply use the terms _____ and maximum.

a. Minimum
b. Ghosts of departed quantities
c. Nth term
d. Maximum

21. The largest and the smallest element of a set are called extreme values, absolute extrema, or extreme records.

For a differentiable function f, if $f(x_0)$ is an _____ for the set of all values f(x), and if x_0 is in the interior of the domain of f, then x_0 is a critical point, by Fermat's theorem.

In the case of a general partial order one should not confuse a least element (smaller than all other) and a minimal element (nothing is smaller.)

Chapter 9. MULTIVARIABLE CALCULUS

a. Infinitesimal
b. Extreme value
c. Integration by substitution
d. Extreme Value Theorem

22. In mathematics, a _____ (or critical number) is a point on the domain of a function where:

- one dimension: the derivative (or slope of the line when visualized) is equal to zero or a point where the function ceases to be differentiable.
- in general: there are two distinct concepts: either the derivative (Jacobian) vanishes, or it is not of full rank (or, in either case, the function is not differentiable); these agree in one dimension.

Note that in one dimension, a critical value or critical number x of function f is the domain element at which the derivative is zero or undefined, whereas the associated ordered pair (x, y) is the _____. In higher dimensions a critical value is in the range whereas a _____ is in the domain.

There are two situations in which a point becomes a _____ of a function of one variable. The first of which is that the value of the first derivative is equal to zero.

a. Critical point
b. Differentiation operator
c. Multivariable calculus
d. Total derivative

23. In mathematics, a _____ is a point in the domain of a function of two variables which is a stationary point but not a local extremum. At such a point, in general, the surface resembles a saddle that curves up in one direction, and curves down in a different direction (like a mountain pass.) In terms of contour lines, a _____ can be recognized, in general, by a contour that appears to intersect itself.
a. BDDC
b. 15 theorem
c. Saddle point
d. BIBO stability

24. In mathematics, _____ and minima, known collectively as extrema, are the largest value (maximum) or smallest value (minimum), that a function takes in a point either within a given neighbourhood (local extremum) or on the function domain in its entirety (global extremum.)

Throughout, a point refers to an input (x), while a value refers to an output (y): one distinguishing between the maximum value and the point (or points) at which it occurs.

A real-valued function f defined on the real line is said to have a local maximum point at the point x*, if there exists some ε > 0, such that f(x*) ≥ f(x) when |x − x*| < ε.

a. Related rates
b. Racetrack principle
c. Leibniz formula
d. Maxima

25. Let f be a differentiable function, and let f'(x) be its derivative. The derivative of f'(x) (if it has one) is written f''(x) and is called the _____ of f. Similarly, the derivative of a _____, if it exists, is written f'''(x) and is called the third derivative of f.

a. Stationary phase approximation
b. Vertical asymptote
c. Slant asymptote
d. Second derivative

26. In calculus, a branch of mathematics, the _____ is a criterion often useful for determining whether a given stationary point of a function is a local maximum or a local minimum.

The test states: If the function f is twice differentiable at a stationary point x, meaning that $f'(x) = 0$, then:

- If $f''(x) < 0$ then f has a local maximum at x.
- If $f''(x) > 0$ then f has a local minimum at x.
- If $f''(x) = 0$, the _____ says nothing about the point x, has a possible inflection point.

In the last case, the function may have a local maximum or minimum there, but the function is sufficiently 'flat' that this is undetected by the second derivative. In this case one has to examine the third derivative. Such an example is f(x) = x⁴.

a. Linearity of differentiation
b. Stationary point
c. Symmetric derivative
d. Second derivative test

27. In mathematical optimization, the method of Lagrange multipliers provides a strategy for finding the maximum/minimum of a function subject to constraints.

Chapter 9. MULTIVARIABLE CALCULUS

For example, consider the optimization problem

$$\text{maximize } f(x, y)$$
$$\text{subject to } g(x, y) = c.$$

We introduce a new variable (λ) called a _____, and study the Lagrange function defined by

$$\Lambda(x, y, \lambda) = f(x, y) - \lambda\Big(g(x, y) - c\Big).$$

If (x,y)≈ is a maximum for the original constrained problem, then there exists a λ such that (x,y,λ)≈ is a stationary point for the Lagrange function (stationary points are those points where the partial derivatives of Λ are zero.) However, not all stationary points yield a solution of the original problem.

a. BIBO stability
b. 15 theorem
c. Lagrange multiplier
d. BDDC

28. The _____ of any solid, liquid, plasma, vacuum or theoretical object is how much three-dimensional space it occupies, often quantified numerically. One-dimensional figures (such as lines) and two-dimensional shapes (such as squares) are assigned zero _____ in the three-dimensional space. _____ is commonly presented in units such as mL or cm^3 (milliliters or cubic centimeters.)

a. Volume
b. Dirac equation
c. Klein-Gordon equation
d. Vector potential

29. Just as the definite integral of a positive function of one variable represents the area of the region between the graph of the function and the x-axis, the _____ of a positive function of two variables represents the volume of the region between the surface defined by the function (on the three dimensional Cartesian plane where z = f(x,y)) and the plane which contains its domain. (Note that the same volume can be obtained via the triple integral -- the integral of a function in three variables -- of the constant function f(x, y, z) = 1 over the above-mentioned region between the surface and the plane.) If there are more variables, a multiple integral will yield hypervolumes of multi-dimensional functions.

a. Trigonometric substitution
b. Constant of integration
c. Risch algorithm
d. Double integral

Chapter 9. MULTIVARIABLE CALCULUS

30. Integration is an important concept in mathematics, specifically in the field of calculus and, more broadly, mathematical analysis. Given a function f of a real variable x and an interval [a, b] of the real line, the _____

$$\int_a^b f(x)\,dx,$$

is defined informally to be the net signed area of the region in the xy-plane bounded by the graph of f, the x-axis, and the vertical lines x = a and x = b.

The term '_____' may also refer to the notion of antiderivative, a function F whose derivative is the given function f.

a. Integral
b. Integrand
c. Indefinite integral
d. Integral test for convergence

31. In infinitesimal calculus, a _____ is traditionally an infinitesimally small change in a variable. For example, if x is a variable, then a change in the value of x is often denoted Δx (or δx when this change is considered to be small.) The _____ dx represents such a change, but is infinitely small.

a. Dirichlet integral
b. The Method of Mechanical Theorems
c. Local maximum
d. Differential

32. In calculus, an _____, primitive or indefinite integral of a function f is a function F whose derivative is equal to f, i.e., F >' = f. The process of solving for antiderivatives is antidifferentiation (or indefinite integration.) Antiderivatives are related to definite integrals through the fundamental theorem of calculus: the definite integral of a function over an interval is equal to the difference between the values of an _____ evaluated at the endpoints of the interval.

a. Indefinite integral
b. Order of integration
c. Antiderivative
d. Integrand

33. The _____ specifies the relationship between the two central operations of calculus, differentiation and integration.

The first part of the theorem, sometimes called the first _____, shows that an indefinite integration can be reversed by a differentiation.

Chapter 9. MULTIVARIABLE CALCULUS

The second part, sometimes called the second _____, allows one to compute the definite integral of a function by using any one of its infinitely many antiderivatives.

   a. Limits of integration
   b. Fundamental Theorem of Calculus
   c. Leibniz formula
   d. Periodic function

34. In calculus, an antiderivative, primitive or _____ of a function f is a function F whose derivative is equal to f, i.e., F ' = f. The process of solving for antiderivatives is antidifferentiation (or indefinite integration.) Antiderivatives are related to definite integrals through the fundamental theorem of calculus: the definite integral of a function over an interval is equal to the difference between the values of an antiderivative evaluated at the endpoints of the interval.
   a. Indefinite integral
   b. Arc length
   c. Integration by parts operator
   d. Integral test for convergence

35. If a function has an integral, it is said to be integrable. The function for which the integral is calculated is called the _____. The region over which a function is being integrated is called the domain of integration.
   a. Order of integration
   b. Integration by parts
   c. Integral test for convergence
   d. Integrand

36. In mathematics, the concept of a '_____' is used to describe the behavior of a function as its argument or input either 'gets close' to some point, or as the argument becomes arbitrarily large; or the behavior of a sequence's elements as their index increases indefinitely. Limits are used in calculus and other branches of mathematical analysis to define derivatives and continuity.

In formulas, _____ is usually abbreviated as lim

   a. BIBO stability
   b. Limit
   c. 15 theorem
   d. BDDC

37. In calculus and mathematical analysis the _____ of the integral

$$\int_a^b f(x)\,dx$$

of a Riemann integrable function f defined on a closed and bounded interval [a, b] are the real numbers a and b.

_____ can also be defined for improper integrals, with the _____ of both

$$\lim_{z \to a+} \int_z^b f(x)\,dx$$

and

$$\lim_{z \to b-} \int_a^z f(x)\,dx$$

again being a and b. For an improper integral

$$\int_a^\infty f(x)\,dx$$

or

$$\int_{-\infty}^b f(x)\,dx$$

the _____ are a and ∞, or −∞ and b, respectively.

a. Maxima
b. Limits of Integration
c. Test for Divergence
d. Differential

Chapter 9. MULTIVARIABLE CALCULUS

38. In elementary algebra, a _____ is a polynomial with two terms--the sum of two monomials--often bound by parenthesis or brackets when operated upon. It is the simplest kind of polynomial other than monomials.

- The _____ $a^2 - b^2$ can be factored as the product of two other binomials:

    $a^2 - b^2 = (a + b)(a - b.)$

    This is a special case of the more general formula:
    $$a^{n+1} - b^{n+1} = (a - b)\sum_{k=0}^{n} a^k b^{n-k}$$

- The product of a pair of linear binomials (ax + b) and (cx + d) is:

    $(ax + b)(cx + d) = acx^2 + axd + bcx + bd.$

- A _____ raised to the nth power, represented as

    $(a + b)^n$
    can be expanded by means of the _____ theorem or, equivalently, using Pascal's triangle. Taking a simple example, the perfect square _____ $(p + q)^2$ can be found by squaring the first digit, adding twice the product of the first and second digit and finally adding the square of the second digit, to give $p^2 + 2pq + q^2$.

a. Multinomial theorem
b. Completing the square
c. Partial fractions
d. Binomial

39. _____ is any physical or virtual entity that is owned by an individual or jointly by a group of individuals. An owner of _____ has the right to consume, sell, rent, mortgage, transfer and exchange his or her _____. Important widely-recognized types of _____ include real _____, personal _____ (other physical possessions), and intellectual _____ (rights over artistic creations, inventions, etc.), although the latter is not always as widely recognized or enforced.
a. BDDC
b. BIBO stability
c. 15 theorem
d. Property

Chapter 10. DIFFERENTIAL EQUATIONS

1. A _____ is a mathematical equation for an unknown function of one or several variables that relates the values of the function itself and of its derivatives of various orders. they play a prominent role in engineering, physics, economics and other disciplines.

   A simplified real world example of a _____ is modeling the acceleration of a ball falling through the air (considering only gravity and air resistance.)

   a. Structural stability
   b. Caloric polynomial
   c. Phase line
   d. Differential equation

2. A _____ officer is an officer of high military rank. The term or equivalent is used by nearly every country in the world. _____ can be used as a generic term for all grades of _____ officer, or it can specifically refer to a single rank that is just called _____.
   a. BDDC
   b. BIBO stability
   c. 15 theorem
   d. General

3. In mathematics, a _____ to an ordinary or partial differential equation is a function for which the derivatives appearing in the equation may not all exist but which is nonetheless deemed to satisfy the equation in some precisely defined sense. There are many different definitions of _____, appropriate for different classes of equations. One of the most important is based on the notion of distributions.
   a. Singular perturbation
   b. Conserved quantity
   c. Structural stability
   d. Weak solution

4. In infinitesimal calculus, a _____ is traditionally an infinitesimally small change in a variable. For example, if x is a variable, then a change in the value of x is often denoted Δx (or δx when this change is considered to be small.) The _____ dx represents such a change, but is infinitely small.
   a. Local maximum
   b. Dirichlet integral
   c. Differential
   d. The Method of Mechanical Theorems

Chapter 10. DIFFERENTIAL EQUATIONS

5. _____ is the concept of adding accumulated interest back to the principal, so that interest is earned on interest from that moment on. The act of declaring interest to be principal is called compounding (i.e., interest is compounded.) A loan, for example, may have its interest compounded every month: in this case, a loan with $100 principal and 1% interest per month would have a balance of $101 at the end of the first month.

    a. Compound interest
    b. BIBO stability
    c. 15 theorem
    d. BDDC

6. In mathematics, in the field of differential equations, an initial value problem is an ordinary differential equation together with specified value, called the _____, of the unknown function at a given point in the domain of the solution. In physics or other sciences, modeling a system frequently amounts to solving an initial value problem; in this context, the differential equation is an evolution equation specifying how, given initial conditions, the system will evolve with time.

An initial value problem is a differential equation

$$y'(t) = f(t, y(t)) \quad \text{with} \quad f : \mathbb{R} \times \mathbb{R} \to \mathbb{R}$$

together with a point in the domain of f

$$(t_0, y_0) \in \mathbb{R} \times \mathbb{R},$$

called the _____.

    a. AUSM
    b. ACTRAN
    c. Initial condition
    d. ALGOR

7. In mathematics, in the field of differential equations, an _____ is an ordinary differential equation together with specified value, called the initial condition, of the unknown function at a given point in the domain of the solution. In physics or other sciences, modeling a system frequently amounts to solving an _____; in this context, the differential equation is an evolution equation specifying how, given initial conditions, the system will evolve with time.

An _____ is a differential equation

$$y'(t) = f(t, y(t)) \quad \text{with} \quad f : \mathbb{R} \times \mathbb{R} \to \mathbb{R}$$

together with a point in the domain of f

$$(t_0, y_0) \in \mathbb{R} \times \mathbb{R},$$

called the initial condition.

    a. ACTRAN
    b. ALGOR
    c. Initial value problem
    d. AUSM

8. In a totally ordered set all elements are mutually comparable, so such a set can have at most one minimal element and at most one maximal element. Then, due to mutual comparability, the minimal element will also be the least element and the maximal element will also be the greatest element. Thus in a totally ordered set we can simply use the terms minimum and _____.

    a. Maximum
    b. Nth term
    c. Leibniz rule
    d. Racetrack principle

9. In calculus, the _____ is a formula for the derivative of the composite of two functions.

In intuitive terms, if a variable, y, depends on a second variable, u, which in turn depends on a third variable, x, then the rate of change of y with respect to x can be computed as the rate of change of y with respect to u multiplied by the rate of change of u with respect to x. Schematically,

$$\frac{dy}{dx} = \frac{dy}{du} \cdot \frac{du}{dx}.$$

    a. Reciprocal Rule
    b. Differentiation rules
    c. Product rule
    d. Chain rule

Chapter 10. DIFFERENTIAL EQUATIONS

10. In mathematics, a _____ differential equation may refer to one of two related things, both of which are differential equations that can be attacked by a method of separation of variables.

- For ordinary differential equations, it describes a class of equations that can be separated into a pair of integrals. See: Examples of differential equations

- For partial differential equations, it describes a class of equations that can be broken down into differential equations in fewer independent variables. See _____ partial differential equation.

a. Method of undetermined coefficients
b. Lax pair
c. Differential equation
d. Separable

11. In mathematics, _____ is any of several methods for solving ordinary and partial differential equations, in which algebra allows one to rewrite an equation so that each of two variables occurs on a different side of the equation.

Suppose a differential equation can be written in the form

$$\frac{d}{dx}f(x) = g(x)h(f(x)), \qquad (1)$$

which we can write more simply by letting y = f(x):

$$\frac{dy}{dx} = g(x)h(y).$$

As long as h(y) ≠ 0, we can rearrange terms to obtain:

$$\frac{dy}{h(y)} = g(x)dx,$$

so that the two variables x and y have been separated.

Some who dislike Leibniz's notation may prefer to write this as

$$\frac{1}{h(y)}\frac{dy}{dx} = g(x),$$

but that fails to make it quite as obvious why this is called '_____'.

a. Power series method
b. Sturm separation theorem
c. Separation of variables
d. Damping ratio

12. _____ is a type of motion in which the velocity of an object changes equal amounts in equal time periods. An example of an object having _____ would be a ball rolling down a ramp. The object picks up velocity as it goes down the ramp with equal changes in time.

a. AUSM
b. ALGOR
c. ACTRAN
d. Uniform Acceleration

13. The _____ of a biological species in an environment is the population size of the species that the environment can sustain in the long term, given the food, habitat, water and other necessities available in the environment. For the human population, more complex variables such as sanitation and medical care are sometimes considered as part of the necessary infrastructure.

As population density increases, birth rate often increases and death rate typically decreases.

a. 15 theorem
b. BDDC
c. BIBO stability
d. Carrying capacity

14. In mathematics, a (topological) _____ is defined as follows: let I be an interval of real numbers (i.e. a non-empty connected subset of $\mathbb{R}$); then a _____ γ is a continuous mapping $\gamma : I \to X$, where X is a topological space. The _____ γ is said to be simple if it is injective, i.e. if for all x, y in I, we have $\gamma(x) = \gamma(y) \implies x = y$. If I is a closed bounded interval $[a, b]$, we also allow the possibility $\gamma(a) = \gamma(b)$ (this convention makes it possible to talk about closed simple _____.)

a. Closed curve
b. Tractrix
c. Prolate cycloid
d. Curve

15. In calculus, the _____ is a formula used to find the derivatives of products of functions. It may be stated thus:

Chapter 10. DIFFERENTIAL EQUATIONS

$$(f \cdot g)' = f' \cdot g + f \cdot g'$$

or in the Leibniz notation thus:

$$\frac{d}{dx}(u \cdot v) = u \cdot \frac{dv}{dx} + v \cdot \frac{du}{dx}.$$

Discovery of this rule is credited to Gottfried Leibniz, who demonstrated it using differentials. Here is Leibniz's argument: Let u and v be two differentiable functions of x.

a. Quotient Rule
b. Differentiation rules
c. Product rule
d. Constant factor rule in differentiation

16. In mathematics, an _____ is a function that is chosen to facilitate the solving of a given ordinary differential equation.

Consider an ordinary differential equation of the form

$$y' + a(x)y = b(x) \qquad (1)$$

where y = y(x) is an unknown function of x, and a(x) and b(x) are given functions.

The _____ method works by turning the left hand side into the form of the derivative of a product.

a. Isomonodromic deformation
b. Oscillating
c. Exponential growth
d. Integrating factor

17. The _____, formerly known as the hyperbolic logarithm, is the logarithm to the base e, where e is an irrational constant approximately equal to 2.718281828. It is also sometimes referred to as the Napierian logarithm, although the original meaning of this term is slightly different. In simple terms, the _____ of a number x is the power to which e would have to be raised to equal x -- for example the natural log of e itself is 1 because e^1 = e, while the _____ of 1 would be 0, since e^0 = 1.

Chapter 10. DIFFERENTIAL EQUATIONS

a. BDDC
b. 15 theorem
c. BIBO stability
d. Natural logarithm

18. In the fields of science, engineering, industry and statistics, _____ is the degree of closeness of a measured or calculated quantity to its actual (true) value. _____ is closely related to precision, also called reproducibility or repeatability, the degree to which further measurements or calculations show the same or similar results. _____ indicates proximity to the true value, precision to the repeatability or reproducibility of the measurement

The results of calculations or a measurement can be accurate but not precise, precise but not accurate, neither, or both.

a. ALGOR
b. AUSM
c. ACTRAN
d. Accuracy

19. The _____ are a pair of first order, non-linear, differential equations frequently used to describe the dynamics of biological systems in which two species interact, one a predator and one its prey. They were proposed independently by Alfred J. Lotka in 1925 and Vito Volterra in 1926.

$$\boxed{x}>$$

$$\boxed{x}>$$

where

- y is the number of some predator;
- x is the number of its prey;
- dy/dt and dx/dt represents the growth of the two populations against time;
- t represents the time; and
- >α, >β, >γ and >δ are parameters representing the interaction of the two species.

When multiplied out, the equations take a form useful for physical interpretation. Their origin should be considered from a more general framework,

where both functions represent per capita growth rates of the prey and predator, respectively.

a. BIBO stability
b. 15 theorem
c. Lotka-Volterra equations
d. BDDC

Chapter 11. PROBABILITY AND CALCULUS

1. _____ is a way of expressing knowledge or belief that an event will occur or has occurred. In mathematics the concept has been given an exact meaning in _____ theory, that is used extensively in such areas of study as mathematics, statistics, finance, gambling, science, and philosophy to draw conclusions about the likelihood of potential events and the underlying mechanics of complex systems.

   The word _____ does not have a consistent direct definition.

   a. Probability
   b. Discrete probability distributions
   c. Linear regression
   d. Normal distribution

2. In probability theory, a probability distribution is called continuous if its cumulative distribution function is continuous. This is equivalent to saying that for random variables X with the distribution in question, Pr[X = a] = 0 for all real numbers a, i.e.: the probability that X attains the value a is zero, for any number a. If the distribution of X is continuous then X is called a _____.

   a. Standard deviation
   b. Probability
   c. Poisson distribution
   d. Continuous random variable

3. In mathematics, a _____ (pdf) is a function that represents a probability distribution in terms of integrals.

   Formally, a probability distribution has density f, if f is a non-negative Lebesgue-integrable function $\mathbb{R} \to \mathbb{R}$ such that the probability of the interval [a, b] is given by

   $$\int_a^b f(x)\,dx$$

   for any two numbers a and b. This implies that the total integral of f must be 1.

   a. Factorial moment generating function
   b. 15 theorem
   c. BDDC
   d. Probability density function

4. In calculus, an _____, primitive or indefinite integral of a function f is a function F whose derivative is equal to f, i.e., F >' = f. The process of solving for antiderivatives is antidifferentiation (or indefinite integration.) Antiderivatives are related to definite integrals through the fundamental theorem of calculus: the definite integral of a function over an interval is equal to the difference between the values of an _____ evaluated at the endpoints of the interval.

a. Indefinite integral
b. Integrand
c. Antiderivative
d. Order of integration

5. The _____ of a material is defined as its mass per unit volume. The symbol of _____ is ρ '>rho.)

Mathematically:

$$d = \frac{m}{V}$$

where:

    d is the _____,
    m is the mass,
    V is the volume.

a. 15 theorem
b. Density
c. BDDC
d. BIBO stability

6. In mathematics, a probability _____ is a function that represents a probability distribution in terms of integrals.

Formally, a probability distribution has density f, if f is a non-negative Lebesgue-integrable function $\mathbb{R} \to \mathbb{R}$ such that the probability of the interval [a, b] is given by

$$\int_a^b f(x)\, dx$$

for any two numbers a and b. This implies that the total integral of f must be 1.

a. Density function
b. Factorial moment generating function
c. 15 theorem
d. BDDC

7. In calculus, an _____ is the limit of a definite integral as an endpoint of the interval of integration approaches either a specified real number or ∞ or -∞ or, in some cases, as both endpoints approach limits.

Specifically, an _____ is a limit of the form

$$\lim_{b \to \infty} \int_a^b f(x)\,dx, \qquad \lim_{a \to -\infty} \int_a^b f(x)\,dx,$$

or of the form

$$\lim_{c \to b^-} \int_a^c f(x)\,dx, \qquad \lim_{c \to a^+} \int_c^b f(x)\,dx,$$

in which one takes a limit in one or the other (or sometimes both) endpoints. Improper integrals may also occur at an interior point of the domain of integration, or at multiple such points.

a. ALGOR
b. ACTRAN
c. AUSM
d. Improper integral

8. Integration is an important concept in mathematics, specifically in the field of calculus and, more broadly, mathematical analysis. Given a function f of a real variable x and an interval [a, b] of the real line, the _____

$$\int_a^b f(x)\,dx,$$

is defined informally to be the net signed area of the region in the xy-plane bounded by the graph of f, the x-axis, and the vertical lines x = a and x = b.

The term '_____' may also refer to the notion of antiderivative, a function F whose derivative is the given function f.

a. Indefinite integral
b. Integral test for convergence
c. Integrand
d. Integral

Chapter 11. PROBABILITY AND CALCULUS

9. In mathematics, a (topological) _____ is defined as follows: let I be an interval of real numbers (i.e. a non-empty connected subset of $\mathbb{R}$); then a _____ γ is a continuous mapping $\gamma : I \to X$, where X is a topological space. The _____ γ is said to be simple if it is injective, i.e. if for all x, y in I, we have $\gamma(x) = \gamma(y) \implies x = y$. If I is a closed bounded interval $[a, b]$, we also allow the possibility $\gamma(a) = \gamma(b)$ (this convention makes it possible to talk about closed simple _____.)

   a. Closed curve
   b. Curve
   c. Prolate cycloid
   d. Tractrix

10. In probability theory and statistics, the _____ (or expectation value or mean and for continuous random variables with a density function it is the probability density -weighted integral of the possible values.

    The term '_____' can be misleading.

    a. Expected value
    b. AUSM
    c. ACTRAN
    d. ALGOR

11. In statistics, _____ is a simple measure of the variability or dispersion of a data set. A low _____ indicates that all of the data points are very close to the same value (the mean), while high _____ indicates that the data is 'spread out' over a large range of values.

    For example, the average height for adult men in the United States is about 70 inches, with a _____ of around 3 inches.

    a. Correlation
    b. Standard deviation
    c. Continuous random variable
    d. Poisson distribution

12. A _____ is a set of standard clothing worn by members of an organization while participating in that organization's activity. Modern uniforms are worn by armed forces and paramilitary organisations such as police, emergency services, security guards, in some workplaces and schools and by inmates in prisons. In some countries, some other officials also wear uniforms in their duties; such is the case of the Commissioned Corps of the United States Public Health Service or the French prefects.

Chapter 11. PROBABILITY AND CALCULUS

a. ALGOR
b. ACTRAN
c. AUSM
d. Uniform

13. The _____ is an important family of continuous probability distributions, applicable in many fields. Each member of the family may be defined by two parameters, location and scale: the mean and variance respectively. The standard _____ is the _____ with a mean of zero and a variance of one.
    a. Moment
    b. Continuous random variable
    c. Normal distribution
    d. Correlation

14. In numerical analysis, _____ constitutes a broad family of algorithms for calculating the numerical value of a definite integral, and by extension, the term is also sometimes used to describe the numerical solution of differential equations The term numerical quadrature is more or less a synonym for _____, especially as applied to one-dimensional integrals.
    a. Multigrid method
    b. Meshfree methods
    c. Galerkin methods
    d. Numerical integration

Chapter 12. SEQUENCES AND SERIES

1. A _____ officer is an officer of high military rank. The term or equivalent is used by nearly every country in the world. _____ can be used as a generic term for all grades of _____ officer, or it can specifically refer to a single rank that is just called _____.
   a. BDDC
   b. General
   c. 15 theorem
   d. BIBO stability

2. In mathematics, a _____ is an ordered list of objects (or events). Like a set, it contains members (also called elements or terms), and the number of terms (possibly infinite) is called the length of the _____. Unlike a set, order matters, and the exact same elements can appear multiple times at different positions in the _____.
   a. 15 theorem
   b. Y-intercept
   c. Slope
   d. Sequence

3. In calculus, a branch of mathematics, the _____ is a measurement of how a function changes when its input changes. Loosely speaking, a _____ can be thought of as how much a quantity is changing at some given point. For example, the _____ of the position (or distance) of a vehicle with respect to time is the instantaneous velocity (respectively, instantaneous speed) at which the vehicle is traveling.

   The process of finding a _____ is called differentiation. The fundamental theorem of calculus states that differentiation is the reverse process to integration.

   a. Stationary phase approximation
   b. Semi-differentiability
   c. Bounded function
   d. Derivative

4. In mathematics, the _____ test for divergence is a simple test for the divergence of an infinite series:

   - If $\lim_{n \to \infty} a_n \neq 0$ or if the limit does not exist, then $\sum_{n=1}^{\infty} a_n$ diverges.

   Many authors do not name this test or give it a shorter name.

Unlike stronger convergence tests, the term test cannot prove by itself that a series converges. In particular, the converse to the test is not true; instead all one can say is:

- If $\lim_{n \to \infty} a_n = 0$, then $\sum_{n=1}^{\infty} a_n$ may or may not converge. In other words, if $\lim_{n \to \infty} a_n = 0$, the test is inconclusive.

The harmonic series is a classic example of a divergent series whose terms limit to zero. The more general class of p-series,

$$\sum_{n=1}^{\infty} \frac{1}{n^p},$$

exemplifies the possible results of the test:

- If p ≤ 0, then the term test identifies the series as divergent.
- If 0 < p ≤ 1, then the term test is inconclusive, but the series is divergent by the integral test for convergence.
- If 1 < p, then the term test is inconclusive, but the series is convergent, again by the integral test for convergence.

The test is typically proved in contrapositive form:

- If $\sum_{n=1}^{\infty} a_n$ converges, then $\lim_{n \to \infty} a_n = 0$.

If s_n are the partial sums of the series, then the assumption that the series converges means that

$$\lim_{n \to \infty} s_n = s$$

for some number s. Then

$$\lim_{n \to \infty} a_n = \lim_{n \to \infty} (s_n - s_{n-1}) = s - s = 0.$$

The assumption that the series converges means that it passes Cauchy's convergence test: for every $\varepsilon > 0$ there is a number N such that

$$\left| a_{n+1} + a_{n+2} + \ldots + a_{n+p} \right| < \varepsilon$$

holds for all n > N and p ≥ 1. Setting p = 1 recovers the definition of the statement

$$\lim_{n \to \infty} a_n = 0.$$

The simplest version of the term test applies to infinite series of real numbers.

a. Slope field
b. Leibniz differential
c. Minimum
d. Nth term

5. A _____ is an expression which compares quantities relative to each other. The most common examples involve two quantities, but in theory any number of quantities can be compared. In mathematical terms, they are represented by separating each quantity with a colon, for example the _____ 2:3, which is read as the _____ 'two to three'.

a. Ratio
b. 15 theorem
c. Sequence
d. Y-intercept

6. In those hierarchically organised churches of Western Christianity which have an ecclesiastical law system, an _____ is an officer of the church who by reason of office has _____ power to execute the church's laws. The term comes from the Latin word ordinarius. In Eastern Christianity, a corresponding officer is called a hierarch, which comes from the Greek word á¼±ερÎ¬ρχης meaning 'priestly ruler'.

a. Ordinary
b. AUSM
c. ACTRAN
d. ALGOR

7. Trigonometry is a branch of mathematics that deals with triangles, particularly those plane triangles in which one angle has 90 degrees (right triangles.) Trigonometry deals with relationships between the sides and the angles of triangles and with the _____ functions, which describe those relationships.

Trigonometry has applications in both pure mathematics and in applied mathematics, where it is essential in many branches of science and technology.

a. Trigonometric
b. Sine
c. Trigonometric integrals
d. Trigonometric functions

8. In mathematics, the _____ are functions of an angle. They are important in the study of triangles and modeling periodic phenomena, among many other applications. _____ are commonly defined as ratios of two sides of a right triangle containing the angle, and can equivalently be defined as the lengths of various line segments from a unit circle.
   a. Trigonometric integrals
   b. Sine integral
   c. Trigonometric functions
   d. Trigonometric

9. _____ is any physical or virtual entity that is owned by an individual or jointly by a group of individuals. An owner of _____ has the right to consume, sell, rent, mortgage, transfer and exchange his or her _____. Important widely-recognized types of _____ include real _____, personal _____ (other physical possessions), and intellectual _____ (rights over artistic creations, inventions, etc.), although the latter is not always as widely recognized or enforced.
   a. 15 theorem
   b. BDDC
   c. BIBO stability
   d. Property

10. In calculus, _____ gives a sequence of approximations of a differentiable function around a given point by polynomials (the Taylor polynomials of that function) whose coefficients depend only on the derivatives of the function at that point. The theorem also gives precise estimates on the size of the error in the approximation. The theorem is named after the mathematician Brook Taylor, who stated it in 1712, though the result was first discovered 41 years earlier in 1671 by James Gregory.
    a. Related rates
    b. Fresnel integrals
    c. Local minimum
    d. Taylor's theorem

11. Cantor defined two kinds of _____ numbers, the ordinal numbers and the cardinal numbers. Ordinal numbers may be identified with well-ordered sets, or counting carried on to any stopping point, including points after an _____ number have already been counted. Generalizing finite and the ordinary _____ sequences which are maps from the positive integers leads to mappings from ordinal numbers, and transfinite sequences.

a. Infinite
b. AUSM
c. ACTRAN
d. ALGOR

12. The terms of the series are often produced according to a certain rule, such as by a formula, by an algorithm, by a sequence of measurements, or even by a random number generator. As there are an infinite number of terms, this notion is often called an _____. Unlike finite summations, series need tools from mathematical analysis to be fully understood and manipulated.
    a. Extreme Value Theorem
    b. Integration by substitution
    c. Extreme value
    d. Infinite series

13. Call S_N the _____ to N of the sequence $\{a_n\}$, or _____ of the series. A series is the sequence of partial sums, $\{S_N\}$.

When talking about series, one can refer either to the sequence $\{S_N\}$ of the partial sums, or to the sum of the series,

$$\sum_{n=0}^{\infty} a_n$$

i.e., the limit of the sequence of partial sums - it is clear which one is meant from context.

   a. The Method of Mechanical Theorems
   b. Dirichlet integral
   c. Maxima
   d. Partial sum

14. In vector calculus, the _____ is an operator that measures the magnitude of a vector field's source or sink at a given point; the _____ of a vector field is a (signed) scalar. For example, consider air as it is heated or cooled. The relevant vector field for this example is the velocity of the moving air at a point.
    a. Green's theorem
    b. Triple product
    c. Divergence
    d. Gradient theorem

Chapter 12. SEQUENCES AND SERIES

15. In mathematics, the _____ of a power series is a non-negative quantity, either a real number or ∞, that represents a domain (within the radius) in which the series will converge. Within the _____, a power series converges absolutely and uniformly on compacta as well. If the series converges, it is the Taylor series of the analytic function to which it converges inside its _____.

   a. Blaschke product
   b. Radius of convergence
   c. Branch point
   d. Holomorphically separable

16. In mathematics, the _____ is a representation of a function as an infinite sum of terms calculated from the values of its derivatives at a single point. It may be regarded as the limit of the Taylor polynomials. If the series is centered at zero, the series is also called a Maclaurin series.

   a. Taylor series
   b. 15 theorem
   c. BIBO stability
   d. BDDC

17. In calculus and other branches of mathematical analysis, an _____ is an algebraic expression obtained in the context of limits. Limits involving algebraic operations are often performed by replacing subexpressions by their limits; if the expression obtained after this substitution does not give enough information to determine the original limit, it is known as an _____. The indeterminate forms include 0^0, $0/0$, 1^∞, $\infty - \infty$, ∞/∞, $0\times\infty$, and ∞^0.

   a. Indeterminate form
   b. AUSM
   c. ACTRAN
   d. ALGOR

18. In mathematics, the concept of a '_____' is used to describe the behavior of a function as its argument or input either 'gets close' to some point, or as the argument becomes arbitrarily large; or the behavior of a sequence's elements as their index increases indefinitely. Limits are used in calculus and other branches of mathematical analysis to define derivatives and continuity.

   In formulas, _____ is usually abbreviated as lim

   a. 15 theorem
   b. BIBO stability
   c. BDDC
   d. Limit

Chapter 13. THE TRIGONOMETRIC FUNCTIONS

1. The _____ of an angle is the ratio of the length of the adjacent side to the length of the hypotenuse. In our case

$$\cos A = \frac{\text{adjacent}}{\text{hypotenuse}} = \frac{b}{h}.$$

The tangent of an angle is the ratio of the length of the opposite side to the length of the adjacent side. In our case

$$\tan A = \frac{\text{opposite}}{\text{adjacent}} = \frac{a}{b}.$$

The remaining three functions are best defined using the above three functions.

a. Sine integral
b. Trigonometric
c. Trigonometric functions
d. Cosine

2. The _____ of an angle is the ratio of the length of the opposite side to the length of the hypotenuse. In our case

$$\sin A = \frac{\text{opposite}}{\text{hypotenuse}} = \frac{a}{h}.$$

Note that this ratio does not depend on size of the particular right triangle chosen, as long as it contains the angle A, since all such triangles are similar.

The cosine of an angle is the ratio of the length of the adjacent side to the length of the hypotenuse.

a. Trigonometric
b. Trigonometric functions
c. Sine integral
d. Sine

3. Trigonometry is a branch of mathematics that deals with triangles, particularly those plane triangles in which one angle has 90 degrees (right triangles.) Trigonometry deals with relationships between the sides and the angles of triangles and with the _____ functions, which describe those relationships.

Trigonometry has applications in both pure mathematics and in applied mathematics, where it is essential in many branches of science and technology.

a. Trigonometric functions
b. Sine
c. Trigonometric integrals
d. Trigonometric

4. In mathematics, the _____ are functions of an angle. They are important in the study of triangles and modeling periodic phenomena, among many other applications. _____ are commonly defined as ratios of two sides of a right triangle containing the angle, and can equivalently be defined as the lengths of various line segments from a unit circle.
   a. Trigonometric functions
   b. Trigonometric integrals
   c. Trigonometric
   d. Sine integral

5. A _____ is a statement of the meaning of a word or phrase. The term to be defined is known as the definiendum . The words which define it are known as the definiens .
   a. Definition
   b. BDDC
   c. 15 theorem
   d. BIBO stability

6. In mathematics, a _____ is a function that repeats its values in regular intervals or periods. The most important examples are the trigonometric functions, which repeat over intervals of length 2π. Periodic functions are used throughout science to describe oscillations, waves, and other phenomena that exhibit periodicity.
   a. Partial sum
   b. Periodic function
   c. Limits of integration
   d. Term test

7. _____ is the magnitude of change in the oscillating variable, with each oscillation, within an oscillating system. For instance, sound waves are oscillations in atmospheric pressure and their amplitudes are proportional to the change in pressure during one oscillation. If the variable undergoes regular oscillations, and a graph of the system is drawn with the oscillating variable as the vertical axis and time as the horizontal axis, the _____ is visually represented by the vertical distance between the extrema of the curve.

a. Amplitude
b. AUSM
c. ALGOR
d. ACTRAN

8. In calculus, a branch of mathematics, the _____ is a measurement of how a function changes when its input changes. Loosely speaking, a _____ can be thought of as how much a quantity is changing at some given point. For example, the _____ of the position (or distance) of a vehicle with respect to time is the instantaneous velocity (respectively, instantaneous speed) at which the vehicle is traveling.

The process of finding a _____ is called differentiation. The fundamental theorem of calculus states that differentiation is the reverse process to integration.

a. Stationary phase approximation
b. Semi-differentiability
c. Derivative
d. Bounded function

9. In a totally ordered set all elements are mutually comparable, so such a set can have at most one minimal element and at most one maximal element. Then, due to mutual comparability, the minimal element will also be the least element and the maximal element will also be the greatest element. Thus in a totally ordered set we can simply use the terms minimum and _____.

a. Racetrack principle
b. Leibniz rule
c. Nth term
d. Maximum

10. In calculus, the _____ is a formula for the derivative of the composite of two functions.

In intuitive terms, if a variable, y, depends on a second variable, u, which in turn depends on a third variable, x, then the rate of change of y with respect to x can be computed as the rate of change of y with respect to u multiplied by the rate of change of u with respect to x. Schematically,

$$\frac{dy}{dx} = \frac{dy}{du} \cdot \frac{du}{dx}.$$

a. Reciprocal Rule
b. Chain rule
c. Product rule
d. Differentiation rules

11. The _____ of any solid, liquid, plasma, vacuum or theoretical object is how much three-dimensional space it occupies, often quantified numerically. One-dimensional figures (such as lines) and two-dimensional shapes (such as squares) are assigned zero _____ in the three-dimensional space. _____ is commonly presented in units such as mL or cm^3 (milliliters or cubic centimeters.)

a. Dirac equation
b. Volume
c. Klein-Gordon equation
d. Vector potential

12. Just as the definite integral of a positive function of one variable represents the area of the region between the graph of the function and the x-axis, the _____ of a positive function of two variables represents the volume of the region between the surface defined by the function (on the three dimensional Cartesian plane where z = f(x,y)) and the plane which contains its domain. (Note that the same volume can be obtained via the triple integral -- the integral of a function in three variables -- of the constant function f(x, y, z) = 1 over the above-mentioned region between the surface and the plane.) If there are more variables, a multiple integral will yield hypervolumes of multi-dimensional functions.

a. Trigonometric substitution
b. Double integral
c. Risch algorithm
d. Constant of integration

13. Integration is an important concept in mathematics, specifically in the field of calculus and, more broadly, mathematical analysis. Given a function f of a real variable x and an interval [a, b] of the real line, the _____

$$\int_a^b f(x)\, dx,$$

is defined informally to be the net signed area of the region in the xy-plane bounded by the graph of f, the x-axis, and the vertical lines x = a and x = b.

The term '_____' may also refer to the notion of antiderivative, a function F whose derivative is the given function f.

Chapter 13. THE TRIGONOMETRIC FUNCTIONS

a. Integral test for convergence
b. Integral
c. Integrand
d. Indefinite integral

14. In mathematics, a (topological) _____ is defined as follows: let I be an interval of real numbers (i.e. a non-empty connected subset of $\mathbb{R}$); then a _____ γ is a continuous mapping $\gamma : I \to X$, where X is a topological space. The _____ γ is said to be simple if it is injective, i.e. if for all x, y in I, we have $\gamma(x) = \gamma(y) \implies x = y$. If I is a closed bounded interval $[a, b]$, we also allow the possibility $\gamma(a) = \gamma(b)$ (this convention makes it possible to talk about closed simple _____.)
   a. Closed curve
   b. Curve
   c. Tractrix
   d. Prolate cycloid

15. If a function has an integral, it is said to be integrable. The function for which the integral is calculated is called the _____. The region over which a function is being integrated is called the domain of integration.
   a. Integration by parts
   b. Order of integration
   c. Integral test for convergence
   d. Integrand

Chapter 1

1. b	2. d	3. d	4. d	5. d	6. c	7. c	8. d	9. d	10. d
11. b	12. d	13. d	14. d	15. b	16. a	17. a	18. b	19. b	20. a
21. d	22. a	23. a							

Chapter 2

1. b	2. b	3. d	4. d	5. d	6. d	7. d	8. d	9. d	10. d
11. b	12. d	13. d	14. d	15. d	16. c	17. b	18. b	19. d	20. d
21. d	22. d	23. d	24. d	25. a	26. d	27. d	28. c	29. a	30. a
31. a	32. d	33. d	34. b	35. a	36. d	37. d	38. b	39. d	40. d
41. b	42. c	43. d							

Chapter 3

1. c	2. d	3. d	4. b	5. d	6. d	7. d	8. b	9. d	10. a
11. d	12. a	13. c	14. d	15. c	16. d	17. d	18. d	19. d	20. d
21. d	22. d	23. d	24. b	25. d					

Chapter 4

| 1. a | 2. b | 3. a | 4. d | 5. d | 6. d | 7. a | 8. d | 9. d | 10. d |
| 11. c | 12. a | 13. d | 14. d | 15. d | 16. d | 17. d | 18. d | 19. a | |

Chapter 5

1. b	2. d	3. c	4. d	5. b	6. b	7. d	8. c	9. a	10. d
11. d	12. b	13. d	14. a	15. c	16. c	17. c	18. a	19. a	20. d
21. d	22. d	23. a	24. d	25. d	26. d	27. d	28. d	29. d	30. d

Chapter 6

| 1. d | 2. d | 3. d | 4. d | 5. d | 6. d | 7. d | 8. b | 9. d | 10. a |
| 11. b | 12. d | 13. d | 14. c | 15. d | 16. d | 17. d | 18. d | 19. b | |

Chapter 7

1. d	2. d	3. d	4. d	5. b	6. c	7. a	8. d	9. d	10. a
11. b	12. d	13. d	14. d	15. d	16. d	17. a	18. c	19. a	20. d
21. d	22. b	23. c	24. d	25. c	26. d	27. d	28. d	29. d	30. c
31. d	32. d								

Chapter 8

| 1. d | 2. d | 3. d | 4. d | 5. b | 6. c | 7. c | 8. b | 9. c | 10. d |
| 11. b | 12. c | 13. d | 14. d | 15. a | 16. c | 17. a | | | |

Chapter 9

1. d	2. c	3. d	4. d	5. d	6. c	7. c	8. c	9. b	10. d
11. d	12. d	13. d	14. a	15. d	16. d	17. d	18. d	19. d	20. a
21. b	22. a	23. c	24. d	25. d	26. d	27. c	28. a	29. d	30. a
31. d	32. c	33. b	34. a	35. d	36. b	37. b	38. d	39. d	

ANSWER KEY

Chapter 10
    1. d   2. d   3. d   4. c   5. a   6. c   7. c   8. a   9. d   10. d
    11. c   12. d   13. d   14. d   15. c   16. d   17. d   18. d   19. c

Chapter 11
    1. a   2. d   3. d   4. c   5. b   6. a   7. d   8. d   9. b   10. a
    11. b   12. d   13. c   14. d

Chapter 12
    1. b   2. d   3. d   4. d   5. a   6. a   7. a   8. c   9. d   10. d
    11. a   12. d   13. d   14. c   15. b   16. a   17. a   18. d

Chapter 13
    1. d   2. d   3. d   4. a   5. a   6. b   7. a   8. c   9. d   10. b
    11. b   12. b   13. b   14. b   15. d

www.ingramcontent.com/pod-product-compliance
Lightning Source LLC
Chambersburg PA
CBHW082048230426
43670CB00016B/2821